THE MASS

Abbreviations

The Mass

Lucien Deiss, C.S.Sp.

Translated by Lucien Deiss, C.S.Sp., and
Michael S. Driscoll

A Liturgical Press Book

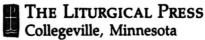 THE LITURGICAL PRESS
Collegeville, Minnesota

Cover design by Greg Becker

Originally published in French by Desclée de Brouwer, 1989

Excerpts from the English translation of *The Roman Missal* © 1973, 1985, International Committee on English in the Liturgy, Inc. (ICEL); excerpts from the *Lectionary for Mass* (second *editio typica*) © 1981, ICEL; excerpts from the *General Instruction of the Roman Missal* (second *editio typica*) from *Documents on the Liturgy, 1963–1979: Conciliar, Papal, and Curial Texts* © 1982, ICEL. All rights reserved.

Library of Congress Cataloging-in-Publication Data

Deiss, Lucien.
    [Messe. English]
    The mass / Lucien Deiss.
        p.   cm.
    Translation of: La messe.
    ISBN 0-8146-2058-2
    1. Mass.   2. Catholic Church—Liturgy.   3. Lord's Supper (Liturgy)
I. Title.
BX2230.2.D45   1992
264'.02036—dc20   92-1217
                                                                  CIP

Contents

Introduction

When the Second Vatican Council spoke about the Mass, it never ceased to celebrate its importance. The Eucharistic celebration is "the center of the Christian community,"[1] "the source and summit of the Christian life,"[2] or further, "the center and culmination of the entire life of the Christian community."[3] Root, source, center, summit: the Eucharistic celebration is at the heart of our faith and our life. To study it is to look at its own heart. That is where we meet Jesus Christ, present in his Word, present in the Eucharist, present in the celebrating community. And it is from the heart of the Mass that this presence radiates into the heart of our life and transfigures it into "eucharist," that is, into thanksgiving.

Two thousand years have clothed this celebration with a cloak of many splendors. All those years have also accumulated layers of dust and introduced practices which, through continual use, have assumed the mask of principles. If the apostles were to attend one of our Masses today, they would have difficulty recognizing the Paschal meal that they celebrated with the Lord in the Upper Room. But in the same way, if Moses had attended the Last Supper of Jesus, would he likewise not have had difficulty recognizing the Pasch that he used to celebrate? That is the law: everything that is living—

---

[1] *Presbyterorum Ordinis*, 5 (Decree on Priestly Ministry and Life).
[2] *Lumen Gentium*, 11 (Constitution on the Church).
[3] *Christus Dominus*, 30 (Decree on the Pastoral Charge of Bishops).

and the liturgical celebration is alive to the highest degree—is in constant evolution.

Certain elements in a cathedral—such as the pillars that support the structure—are essential, one could say constitutive; they cannot be taken away without the entire edifice collapsing. Other parts—such as the statues, for example,—are accessories, sometimes simply decorations: they can be moved, replaced, taken away, or even placed in a museum of memories without infringing on the solidity of the edifice. In the cathedral of the Eucharistic celebration, Vatican II restored and disentangled the constitutive elements—the pillars—of the celebration. The structure of the celebration now appears simpler, more luminous, more beautiful. Vatican II also removed the dust from the accessory parts—the statues—by restoring some and by placing others in the museum of memories. It also unmasked certain practices which had inserted themselves in the liturgy as laws and dominated the celebration.

We are looking at the Mass as the Council restored it. We shall keep an open and admiring eye on all its splendor. We shall also visit the museum of memories. We know that no reform is perfect and that the liturgy, like the Church itself, remains subject to the law that the Council with boldness and magnificence called *perennis reformatio*, permanent reform.[4]

---

[4] *Unitatis Redintegratio,* 6 (Decree on Ecumenism).

General Structure of the Mass

When following the rites of the Mass step by step, we sometimes risk becoming bogged down in details and not noticing the general structure of the Mass. What is that structure?

Throughout the ages, people have been able to underline sometimes the sacrificial aspect (the Mass is the memorial of the sacrifice of the cross), other times the Eucharistic aspect (the Mass is the thanksgiving of the Christian community), still other times the real Presence (the presence of Christ in the Eucharistic bread and wine), and sometimes even the ceremonial splendor (in imitation of the royal courts, the Mass is the celebration of the heavenly King). Each one of these aspects possesses an element of truth; they correspond to the theological concerns of the various ages. But if one could abstract from the fluctuations of history, what would one say when referring only to Scripture?

When Jesus celebrated the first Eucharist, he said: "This is the blood of the New Covenant."[5] Therefore Jesus refers explicitly to the Old Covenant,[6] the one that Moses proclaimed on Sinai when he said: "This is the blood of the Covenant that Yahweh has made with you" (Exod 24:8).

[5] "This cup is the new Covenant in my blood" (Luke 22:20).

[6] Exod 24:3-11 describes the conclusion of the Covenant not as it took place on the historical level, but as tradition reconstructed it from different sources. See the analysis of D. Dore, *Le point théologique*, 24, Beauchesne, 1977, pp.147–171 which envisions the rite of the Covenant "on the level of a global reading of ch. 24 of the Exodus" (p. 168).

The Celebration of the Covenant of Sinai

The celebration of this Covenant includes, on the one hand, the proclamation of the Word and its acceptance by the people: "Moses took the Book of the Covenant and read it to the people who declared: 'Everything that Yahweh has said we will do, and we will obey'" (Exod 24:7).

On the other hand, it includes the *sacrifice of the Covenant,* that is, the sacrifice of victims (Exod 24:5) and the meal of communion: "They saw God. They ate and they drank" (Exod 24:11).

These two elements, the celebration of the Word and the sacrifice of the Covenant, are intimately bound in the sense that the celebration of the Word is the foundation upon which the Covenant is built. Moses says: "This is the blood of the *Covenant that Yahweh has made with you in accordance with all these words"* (Exod 24:8).

The Celebration of the New Covenant

Like the celebration at Sinai, the celebration of the New Covenant includes, on the one hand, the proclamation of God's Word: "Jesus taught in the synagogues and proclaimed the Good News of the Kingdom" (Matt 4:23).

On the other hand, it includes the sacrifice of the Covenant, that is, the death and resurrection of Jesus and the communion meal: "Take and eat. This is my body . . . which is given for you . . . This cup is the New Covenant in my blood."[7]

As in the Covenant of Sinai, Word and sacrifice are intimately joined. Jesus dies for the Good News that he proclaims. And the apostles receive the body which is given for them, the blood which is poured out for the many.[8]

The Mass of the Christian Community

As the Old Covenant celebrated by Moses, or as the New Covenant celebrated by Jesus, the Mass of the Christian community in-

[7] We have regrouped here Matt 26:26 and Luke 22:19-20.
[8] Matt 26:26-28.

cludes both the celebration of the Word—the readings of each Mass—and the celebration of the sacrifice of Jesus, that is, the memorial of his death and his resurrection, as well as the meal of communion in the reception of the Eucharistic bread and wine. These two parts are intimately bound and, each one for its part, is constitutive of the Covenant. In each Mass the words of Moses resound: "This is the blood of the Covenant that Yahweh made with you in accordance with all these words." Vatican II sums up this teaching in this way: The two parts which in a sense constitute the Mass, that is, the Liturgy of the Word and the Liturgy of the Eucharist, are so closely connected with each other that they form one single act of worship.[9]

This *single act of worship* is the celebration of the Covenant. The Christian community joyfully has accepted the changes that the Council introduced into the celebration of the Eucharist. But it especially noticed the newness of the readings of the Word of God. It welcomed this newness with enthusiasm. It progresses—sometimes with a certain slowness—in the true tradition of the Church which is to venerate the Word as much as the Eucharist. That is really what Vatican II teaches: "The Church has always venerated the divine Scriptures as it venerated the Body of the Lord."[10]

On this path of veneration, there still remains a long road to travel. But it is a road of wonder, for, like the disciples of Emmaus, we travel with Christ.

We have added some technical references to our study. They are not meant to encumber the reader.[11] They are given simply because honesty obligates us to indicate precisely the sources used. We would like the reader to travel the same path of wonder that we did, and, if he or she desires, to arrive at the same conclusions.

Lucien Deiss, C.S.Sp.

---

[9] *Sacrosanctum Concilium*, 56 (Decree on the Sacred Liturgy).
[10] *Dei Verbum*, 21 (Constitution on Divine Revelation).
[11] A glossary of technical terms can be found at the back of this volume.

Part One
Introductory Rites

The Entrance Song

The celebration of the "summit of the Christian life" begins with a song.

Moreover, there are many songs in the Mass. Formerly, singing was confined to very precise rubrical channels. Today, with new avenues being explored, singing stretches out more freely throughout the celebration.

By singing at Mass, we find ourselves following tradition. People were already singing at the first Mass. Telling about the Paschal meal, Matt 26:30 and Mark 14:26 note that Jesus sang hymns (hymnēsantes) with his apostles. They were singing songs of the Hallel, that is, Pss 113 to 118, which concluded the Paschal meal.

In Rome, the Entrance Song itself seems to go back to the middle of the sixth century (according to Ordo I which dates, no doubt, from the end of the seventh century).[1] At that time it consisted of an antiphon (Antiphona ad Introitum) which was alternated with the verses of a psalm.

It is here that we can ask the question of what is called the "ministerial function," the fundamental question that concerns all

---

[1] The Ordo (understood: missae) is the book which describes the order to be followed for the celebration of the Mass as well as the details of the ceremonies. The oldest Ordo known is the Ordo Antiquus Gallicanus (Regensburg: Ed. Pustet, 1965) from the sixth century. The most recent is the one promulgated April 6, 1969, after Vatican II.

the songs and even all the rites of the liturgy. *The Constitution on the Sacred Liturgy* (art. 112) and the Instruction on Music in the Liturgy of March 5, 1967 (art. 1 and 2) affirm that music called "sacred" fulfills a *munus ministeriale*, literally a "ministerial ministry," a *ministerial function* as it is generally translated. What does that mean?

The word *munus* means duty, function, office. The adjective *ministeriale* comes from *munus*. The ministerial function of the reader is to read. The ministerial function of the chalice is to hold the consecrated wine. What is the ministerial function of a song? To ask that question is to ask the very simple question a child would ask when confronted with an unfamiliar object: "Tell me what do you use that for?" What is the ministerial function of the Entrance Song? For it is clear that we were not baptized to sing Entrance Songs.

The question of the ministerial function—"What do we use that for?"—strikes at the root of the rite or the song. For it is clear that if something does not serve any purpose, or if it is at cross-purposes, the rite or the song must be cut at its root.

Tradition, through the aid of the Magisterium and also through good Christian common sense, discovered and underlined several ministerial functions[2]: singing is an element of solemnization (people sing in solemn Masses), it clothes the celebration with beauty (which is the essential duty of all art and especially of music), it expresses the unity of the celebrating community. It is principally this function of unification that the Entrance Song fulfills. The Instruction on *Music in the Liturgy* (art. 5) affirms: "The unity of hearts is more profoundly achieved by the union of voices." As long as Michael, John, Monica and Jane met outside of the Church—let us be precise: outside of the Church building they formed the Body of Christ, but in an invisible manner. They remained dispersed in their multiple personal occupations; sometimes they barricaded themselves in their individual royal autonomy. Now when they gather together in the Church, they form the visible Body of Christ; as Vatican II

---

[2] See L. Deiss, *Spirit and Song of the New Liturgy*, (Cincinnati: World Library Publications, Inc., 1970), pp. 13–20, where one will find all the texts of the Magisterium.

says, they manifest "the visible Church established in the universe."[3]
The Entrance Song is the first expression of that visible unity.

To sum up: at the beginning of the Mass, we sing to express
the unity of the community and because singing clothes the celebration with beauty. But if the quality of the singing does not surpass
the quality of the silence that it claims to fill, or if it divides the
community—on one side the choir or soloist, who sing, and on the
other side the mute faithful, who listen, it is preferable to be silent.
How many beautiful occasions for being quiet have been lost in
the new liturgy, or even have been polluted by mediocre songs! And

---

The Beginning of Easter Mass in 426
at Hippo, at the Time of Saint Augustine

Paul and Palladia, brother and sister, were miraculously cured right
before the Easter Mass on Sunday morning. Augustine relates:

> On all sides, the church was filled with cries of joy and thanksgiving.
> People ran to the place where I was sitting, already ready to come
> forward. Each one hurried after the other, the last one telling me as
> new what the first had already told me. Quite joyous, I gave thanks
> to God in myself when the young man himself arrived, well surrounded; he threw himself at my knees and arose to receive my kiss.
> We came forward toward the people. The church was full; it resounded with cries of joy: Thanks be to God! Praise be to God! No
> one stays quiet; from the right, from the left, rose up cries!
> I greeted the people. The acclamation started again with redoubled
> intensity.
> Finally silence was established, and the passage from the Holy
> Scriptures was read which dealt with the feast.

> The City of God, 22,8,22.
> Trans. G. Brady. *Oeuvres de Saint Augustin*, 37
> (1960), p. 593.
> Cf. R. Cabié, *The Eucharist*, pp. 50–51.

---

[3] *Constitution on the Sacred Liturgy (Sacrosanctum Concilium)*, 42.

how many magnificent celebrations have occurred when rite and song fully attained their ministerial function!

Ordo I notes that the singing of the Entrance Song, Hymn, or Psalm begins when the ministers begin to enter and that it ends when the procession is finished.[4] When the priest, representing Christ, joins the celebrating community, the Church, the Body of the risen Lord, with its head and its members, is signified in its totality.

The First Gesture of the Priest

The first gesture of the priest is the veneration of the altar: he bows before the altar and kisses it.

The altar is not only "the center of thanksgiving,"[5] the table where the "Lord's Supper" (1 Cor 11:20) is celebrated, but at the same time the sign of Jesus Christ in the midst of the community. Tradition affirms *Altare Christus est*, "the altar is Christ."[6]

Kissing the altar is a gesture of veneration and tender respect. At the same time it expresses an attitude of adoration toward Christ. In antiquity, people brought their hand to their mouth *(ad-os)* to send a kiss to someone, or they even brought the edge of the garment of the person they wanted to honor to their mouth (a gesture still used in the East). A graffiti on the Palatine in Rome (which was an army barracks) which is meant to ridicule the Christian faith shows someone sending a kiss to a man with a head of a donkey, hanging on a cross, with the caption: "Alexamenos adores (literally: venerates the divinity of) his God." Farther away is also found the signature: "Alexamenos (remains) faithful."

The priest is going to direct the celebration, but first before the entire community he manifests his love and his adoration toward Christ the Lord who seduced his heart. The priest himself is only a servant among many others: he simply assumes a particular ministry, the one of presidency.

[4] R. Cabié, *The Eucharist, The Church at Prayer 2* (Collegeville: The Liturgical Press, 1986), p. 51. All the technical references will be found in this work translated from the French edition.

[5] *General Instruction of the Roman Missal*, 259.

[6] *Ordo dedicationis Ecclesiae et altaris*, 4,4.

The First Word of the Priest

The priest begins by greeting the assembly. Three formulas are proposed. The first, in a Trinitarian form, is borrowed from 2 Cor 13:14:

> The grace of our Lord Jesus Christ
> and the love of God
> and the fellowship of the Holy Spirit
> be with you all.

The two other formulas are Christological. The second one is borrowed from Eph 1:2:

> The grace and peace of God our Father
> and the Lord Jesus Christ
> be with you.

The third formula is the traditional "The Lord be with you." This greeting is repeated two more times in the celebration: once to introduce the praise of the Preface and a last time before the final blessing. One would think that it is the most banal formula. Actually it is the most meaningful. In reality it expresses the very mystery of Jesus, Emmanuel, that is, "God with us."

At the beginning of his Gospel, Matthew underlined the mystery of Christ: "They will call him Emmanuel, which is translated: 'God with us.'" (1:23). And at the end of his Gospel, Matthew affirms this mystery once again: Jesus says, "I am with you all the days until the end of time" (28:20). The entire life of Jesus and the entire message of his Gospel are summed up in this double affirmation of the presence of Emmanuel. These two affirmations are like the two pillars upon which rests the arch that allows the community to go from the birth of Jesus to his resurrection. By affirming in the same way the mystery of Emmanuel at the beginning and at the end of the Mass, the liturgy affirms that the entire Eucharistic celebration is founded on Emmanuel, and that the community, transfigured into the Body of Christ, becomes in its turn "Emmanuel" for the world.

If the Lord is with the celebrating community in this way, we can answer the following two questions. Who celebrates the Mass? Formerly, one would answer: the priest. Today we answer: the community with its priest, each one celebrating at his or her own level. Second question: Who presides over the celebration? Formerly, one would answer: the priest. Today we answer: Christ.

Concerning this matter let us notice that the first edition of the new Order of Mass in 1969 spoke about the "celebrant" to signify the priest as if the community itself was not also celebrating. The second edition in 1970 fortunately corrected this confusion, and to designate the priest it said *sacerdos celebrans*, the priest celebrant.[7] There is proof that a very official text is capable of converting into sound theology in one year.

The Penitential Preparation

The entire Church, down to its most sinful members, is holy, "pure and immaculate" (Eph 5:27). She is holy with the very holiness of Jesus. She is without sin, but not without sinners. Her holiness consists precisely in recognizing herself a sinner in order to be able to welcome the forgiveness of Jesus. Therefore it is normal that the Christian celebration include the recognition and forgiveness of sins. When Yahweh reveals himself to Isaiah in the glory of the Temple and calls him to his service, the prophet groans: "Woe to me, I am lost, for I am a man of unclean lips" (Isa 6:4). When Jesus invites Peter to leave the fish of his lake and to follow him, Peter sighs: "Go away from me, for I am a sinner" (Luke 5:8). When the community enters into the celebration, it likewise beseeches:

> Lord, we have sinned against you.
> Lord, show us your mercy and love.

The Ordo proposes a choice of several forms for penitential preparation. The most common is the *Kyrie eleison*, which is in Greek.

The origin of the *Kyrie* is lost in the mist that covers the ancient liturgy. It is thought that the three *Kyrie*, *Christe*, and *Kyrie* were fixed in the eighth century. Originally, the invocations were

---

[7] See *Enchiridion Documentorum Instaurationis Liturgiae*, Marietti, 1976, p. 483.

addressed to Christ. Then they were given a Trinitarian orientation: the first *Kyrie* was supposed to be addressed to the Father,
the *Christe* naturally to Christ, and the last *Kyrie* to the Holy Spirit.
The liturgical reform gave back to the *Kyrie* its Christological
dimension.

Prayer of the Kyrie
at the evening service at the Church of the Resurrection,
in Jerusalem circa 381/382

When the people finish saying the Psalms and the antiphons according to custom, the bishop rises and stands before the grill, that
is, in front of the grotto. One of the deacons commemorates the persons, as is the custom. At each name, children who are standing
there, in great number, constantly respond *Kyrie eleison*, which we
say: *Lord, have mercy*, and their voices are innumerable.

Egeria's Travels, 24,4 (London, SPCK, 1971).

This penitential preparation calls to mind both the private prepa-
rations that the ministers made before beginning the celebration,
a preparation in which the people would have liked to share, or
further the "apologies" or protestations of unworthiness and repen-
tance that have invaded all the liturgies and in which the priest affirms aloud that he is miserable. Why was this penitential rite not
always received with great fervor in liturgical milieux and why did
it enter into the Mass only after considerable discussions?[8]
   It is not the recognition of sins that dulls celebration. It is the
superabundance of penitential formulas which invade the Mass and
break the rhythm of the celebration. Be the judge: The community
begins with the Confiteor. In it the community recognizes that it
has sinned a great deal in thought, in word, through actions and

---

[8] See B. Botte, *Le mouvement liturgique* (Paris: Desclée, 1973), p. 180.

through omission. It insists: "Yes, I have sinned exceedingly." The priest then declares forgiveness on the part of God: "May almighty God have mercy on us, forgive us our sins, and bring us to everlasting life." One then thinks that everything is settled and forgiven.

—Not at all. As if nothing had taken place, one puts everything back into question and begins again to implore the Lord once more for mercy in the *Kyrie:* "Lord, have mercy."

—One enters then into the joy of the *Gloria.* But a new penitential cloud arises in the heaven of praise. One sings: "Lamb of God, you take away the sin of the world, have mercy on us."

—One takes advantage of the washing of hands to beseech again: "Lord, wash away my iniquity; cleanse me from my sin."

—In the Lord's Prayer, we pray as Jesus asked us: "Forgive us our trespasses as we forgive those who trespass against us."

—In the prayer before Communion, we insist once again: "Lord Jesus Christ. . . . By your holy body and blood free me from all my sins," and further: "Let it [Communion] not bring me condemnation, but health in mind and body."

—This prayer is directly linked to the one of the Lamb of God who, once again, takes away the sin of the world.

Enough is enough!

And just as one cannot always repeat the same gestures with the same truth, the penitential prayer is sometimes lowered to the level of a simple rite: that is the supreme humiliation that a prayer can suffer.

Let us notice that the old ritual of the Mass had even heavier formulas. The prayer of the offertory, *Suscipe, sancte Pater,* conveyed: "Receive, holy Father . . . this immaculate offering that I, your unworthy servant, offer to you for my innumerable sins, offenses, and negligences."

Entering into the church of Saint-Etienne-du-Mont, at the Place Sainte Geneviève in Paris, I was astounded by that symphony of stones. It is a marvel of proportion and harmony. I also admired the chapels on the sides. In each chapel was a confessional. The confessionals were enormous, in sculptured wood, with three seats! I counted eight in all. Enough is enough! But these confessionals clearly give a certain vision of the Church which formerly used to delight in recognizing herself a sinner.

The excess of the penitential formulas—like the excess of the confessionals—risks disfiguring both the image of the Church and of its celebration.

Instead of being the joyous thanksgiving of the community risen with Christ, the celebration risks being transformed into individual and collective lamentation.

How, then, should we celebrate the penitential rite so that it does not become a tearful and moralizing introspection of guilt? We should transform it into an acclamation to the mercy of God.

In fact, the heart of the celebration of forgiveness is not the penitential preparation but the celebration of the Eucharist itself. It is in the words of the consecration that Jesus declares to us his forgiveness and gives it to us: "This is the cup of my blood, the blood of the new and everlasting covenant. It will be shed for you and for all so that sins may be forgiven." There is the forgiveness for which we give thanks in the Eucharist. The confession itself is not so much the confession-recognition of our sins, but rather the confession-recognition of the forgiving mercy of God, the praise of his love, the acclamation of his salvation. The penitential preparation is not a type of doormat where we wipe our feet before entering the sanctuary of God's holiness. Rather, it is already thanksgiving for the forgiveness that we never cease to receive. The Missal explains: [The *Kyrie*] is a song by which the faithful praise the Lord and implore his mercy." What must be understood is: "The *Kyrie* is a song by which the faithful praise . . . his mercy."⁹

Greek "Kyrie" or "Lord, have mercy"

The translation "Lord, have mercy," "Christ, have mercy" is not a marvel. It has been rightly criticized and equivalents have been

---

⁹ *General Instruction of the Roman Missal*, 30.

sought.(The German, Italian, Spanish, and French translations are hardly any better.) To tell the truth, I do not find these translations to be less euphonic than the Greek *Kyrie eleison*, which involves the sound *a* three times. Nevertheless I am sorry for these translations and prefer unquestionably the Greek *Kyrie*. Let me explain.

At the end of the Council, the wave of living language unfurled on the shores of the liturgy with such violence and such spontaneity that it swept away almost all the texts in a dead language. It only spared a few islets like the Hebrew *Amen, Alleluia, Hosanna*. Perhaps one may explain this as a reaction against the tyranny that Latin used to exercise with regard to the language of the people. However, it can be said that the *Kyrie* cannot be confused with some Latin text and that it deserves to remain in the liturgy. Indeed, in the Mass, this text is the only text of the language of the Gospels: it is the humble prayer of the two blind men begging for light (Matt 9:29), it is the tumultuous imploring of Bartimaeus on the road to Jericho (Mark 10:47-48), it is the audacious prayer of the Canaanite woman for her little girl (Matt 15:22). The litany of the *Kyrie* is the litany of human misery imploring the mercy of Jesus on Galilean roads. Can it not remain the litany of our misery on the road of our life? The *Kyrie* also represents symbolically the presence of the Church of the East in the Roman liturgy: it is even the only Greek prayer that the people know. I know that these arguments are of an affective order, for one can implore the mercy of Jesus in all the languages of the world and pray with our brothers and sisters of the Eastern Churches in English as well as in Greek. But the affective order also has its merits.

Glory to God in the Highest

With the hymn *Joyous Light* (*phōs hilaron*) and *Praise to You* (*Te decet laus*), the *Gloria* belongs to the most ancient hymns that Christian piety had written in honor of Jesus Christ. The Eastern liturgy calls it "The Great Doxology," as opposed to the little doxology (Glory to the Father, and to the Son, and to the Holy Spirit) with which one ordinarily ends the Psalms.

According to Saint Athanasius (373) and the *Apostolic Constitutions,* the *Gloria* originally appeared in the praise of morning prayer.[10] The beginning takes up the hymn of the angels at the birth of Jesus in Bethlehem. That is why the bishops integrated it into the Christmas Mass towards the sixth century. And since priests always like to imitate bishops, they integrated it into their own Masses: this was done in the eighth century. Thus this song entered into the Eucharistic liturgy.

This hymn is one of the most beautiful in Christian tradition. Its beauty is resplendent not so much in its literary composition—it is primarily the Greek text that bears witness to it, and no translation can restore the flame of that rhythmic prose—but rather in its praise of God. The Father, the source of all blessing, predestined us "before the creation of the world" to be in his presence, in the eternity of his love, living "praises of glory" (Eph 1:3-6). By singing *Glory to God* at the beginning of Mass, by praising his glory, we pronounce our own name; we unite with the angels to proclaim this glory: "We worship you, we give you thanks [*eucharistoumen*, 'we make eucharist'], we praise you for your glory." Like a bouquet of flowers of the most diverse and most glistening colors, the *Gloria* gathers together different forms of human prayer into a sheaf of praise. We glorify God as in the Preface, we give him thanks (*eucharistoumen*) as in the Eucharistic Prayer, we implore his forgiveness as in the penitential preparation, we celebrate his holiness—"You alone are the Holy One," as in the *Sanctus.* We ask in a general way: "Receive our prayer." But the dominant note in this symphony is the jubilation of praise. We begin with "Glory to God" and we end with a type of inclusion with "in the glory of God the Father"; like two hands gather together a bouquet, all the different prayers are gathered together in this double glorification of God.

As doxology, the *Gloria* belongs to the highest form of Christian prayer. Before the transcendence of the Father who is celebrated by angelic multitudes, before the marvels of salvation that God manifests in the midst of his people, before the Eucharist that makes the risen Lord dwell in the heart of the poverty of the celebrating

---

[10] See L. Deiss, *Spirit and Song of the New Liturgy,* pp. 192–195.

community, what can we do except repeat "Glory to you, O Lord!" We know well that we can add nothing to the infinity of this glory, whatever the splendor of our song may be, whatever the stammering of our prayer may be. But we also know that our human nobleness consists precisely in acclaiming the nobleness of God, in opening ourselves up to the radiance of this glory through the Amen of our soul. It is here, for the first time since the beginning of the Mass, that the community enters fully into the sacerdotal celebration to which it is called: "You are a royal priesthood, a holy nation, a chosen people, in order to proclaim the praises of the One who has called you out of darkness to his wonderful light (1 Pet 2:9).

"Sacred" Music?

The *Gloria* is a hymn: that is the way the General Instruction presents it.[11] As such, it is suitable to sing it. For a song is a song only if it is sung: that is a rule of simple common sense. The *Gloria* should never be "recited" any more than anyone would recite the song "Happy Birthday to you." Besides, it is only used in a context of great solemnity.

There are many other songs in the Mass. In short, the following question can be asked: What, then, is the music that we call sacred?

A teaching Sister whom I had met at a workshop and whom I had asked what she taught answered me with a smile: "I teach Catholic mathematics." I understood that she taught math in a Catholic institution. The question can be asked: Is there Catholic music? Christian melodies? Pious rhythm? Sacred music?

In the past, one spoke freely—especially since the nineteenth century—about sacred music. The expression is found in Pius X, *Tra le sollecitudini* (1903), in the encyclical of Pius XII, *Musicae sacrae disciplina* (1955), and in his instruction *De musica sacra* (1958). But history reveals that the expression is ambiguous; the very idea of music that would be sacred is fragile. The masters of the Renaissance, from Josquin des Pres (†1521) to Lassus (†1594), used the same ink to write a very pious Mass and a light-hearted

---

[11] *General Instruction of the Roman Missal*, 31.

madrigal. J. S. Bach himself (†1750), honorable Christian that he was, used a melody that he had composed for a profane cantata in his famous *Bereite dich Zion* of the Oratorio for Christmas. Luther (†1546), who understood music very well, wrote many choral texts on profane melodies. The Christmas chorale *Es kam ein Engel hell und klar* was written on the melody of a popular dance. Luther claimed that it was not good for the devil to have the beautiful melodies for himself alone. The most famous chorale of the Passion *O Haupt voll Blut und Wunden* comes from a lively song by Hans Leo Hassler (1564–1612) which appeared in a collection entitled "Garden of Pleasure of New German Dances." Its lyrics, which were quite affirmed: "My feelings are led astray by a tender virgin" (*Mein G'müt ist mir verwirret von einer Jungfrau zart*). J. S. Bach[12] plucked the melody in the "garden of pleasure" and replanted it in the enclosure of the Church, took it out of its waltz rhythm of three-four time by imposing a meditative and majestic four-four time upon it and clothed it with a sumptuous harmonic garment which still touches our heart today. Therefore, there is no sacred music. Or rather, all music can enter into the service of God if it accepts "conversion."

Let us also note that "sacred" music is not necessarily liturgical music. Bach's Mass in C Minor cannot be used in a Eucharistic celebration, and his *Magnificat* has no place in the Evening Office: yet both are marvels of beauty and religious expression. That same thing can be said about certain pieces of classic polyphony: even though clothed with a thousand splendors, a *Sanctus* from a Mass of Palestrina (†1594) or of Vittoria (†1611) is not suitable for a liturgical celebration simply because, according to the liturgy, the *Sanctus* must be the acclamation of the entire assembly.

Rather than speak about sacred music, today it is preferable to speak about "ritual or service music" or "music of the Christian liturgy."[13] That is the music that fulfills its ministerial function for which it was arranged. Thus the *Ita Missa est* from the Gregorian Mass *Fons bonitatis*, in spite of the melodic splendor of its thirty-

[12] According to A. Schweitzer, *J.S. Bach* (Wiesbaden: Breitkopf & Härtel, 1952), p. 16.

[13] See Duchesneau-Veuthey, *Musique et Liturgie*, Coll. "Rites et symboles," 17 (1988), pp. 23 and 130–133.

four notes which unfold like a festive garland, is little suited to its ministerial function, whereas the three notes of "Go in the peace of Christ," in spite of the humility of the melody, are well-adapted to their ministerial function because they state clearly what they want to say.

Necessary Beauty

Art—music and singing—is the flower of beauty. It creates an environment of splendor. It opens a path to God. The General Instruction notes in this regard that everything that serves in the liturgy must be "truly worthy and beautiful, signs and symbols of heavenly realities."[14] Vatican II should have marked the banishment of all music that is not beautiful or that is not well executed . . . If only it had!

The danger of estheticism remains. It unceasingly threatens to invade the peace of our celebrations. It is the temptation to seek beauty for itself when it is simply a path to God. There is the danger of the choir which, instead of serving the celebrating community, becomes intoxicated with its own harmonies or rhythms—whether this is in the Palestrina, Gregorian, or guitar genre does not change the problem. There is the danger of architecture that makes grandiloquent rhetoric in large flows of concrete or audacious pseudo-Gothic arches instead of creating first a place for the assembly. There is the danger of vestments which instead of having that first beauty which is to be an attire for prayer, disguise the priest into a prince in an operetta and the children of the sanctuary into mini princes. Patiently, we must elude the temptations of estheticism and put beauty back into the service of prayer.

One could ask how the General Instruction, which has so many excellent points, could affirm: "There is also the ancient proverb: 'One who sings well prays twice.' "[15] What naiveté! What about those who do not sing well? Or those who do not sing at all? And which one of us would dare to admit that he or she has never been seduced by the beauty of the music to the point of forgetting to

[14] *General Instruction of the Roman Missal,* 253.
[15] *General Instruction of the Roman Missal,* 19.

pray? Of course, it is necessary to pray while singing. But it is also possible to sing very well and not pray at all. And the best performing choirs are not necessarily the most prayerful.

In truth, music, like all created beauty, is a path to God. It is not a dwelling to remain in forever. Like all creation, it is simply a loan of God's love on the road to heaven. The beauty of music is loaned to us as is loaned to us the laughter of the flute, the call of the trumpet, the outburst of great organs, or even the perfume of a rose blooming on the altar, the smile of a child, or the grace of a girl. The bread of the earth is also loaned to us so that we might transform it into bread of heaven, into Eucharist, into thanksgiving, into praise of the Father. That is really how the singing of the *Gloria* must open us to heavenly praise: only grace—and not music—can open this path for us and bring about this transfiguration.

The Prayer or the Collect

The Introductory Rites end with a prayer which is also called the Collect.

The unfolding of this presidential prayer is as follows:

—An invitation to prayer.

—A time of silence during which all presents their intentions to God.

—The presidential prayer in which the priest "collects" the prayers of all into one prayer.

The structure of this prayer itself is as follows:

—The invocation: God . . .

—The anamnesis or thanksgiving: Who . . .

—The request: Give . . .

—The affirmation of the mediation of Christ: Through Christ.[16]

The text of these prayers poses a problem. In the liturgical reform, things were done in a hurry. The official Latin was some-

---

[16] For example, of the 1030 prayers in the Leonine Sacramentary (sixth century), all, except for about two, end with these short clauses.

times translated into an elegant and thoroughbred version. Those texts conveyed a theology that was certainly perfectly suited to the sensibility of the sixth century. They also raised up an old literary esthetic, often ending with *cursus* (that is, rhythmic unities) that balanced the Latin phrase pleasantly, sometimes proposing a play on words which should have delighted those who spoke Latin but which no translation could render. (For example: *celebrando proficere, proficiendo celebrare*, that is, "to progress while celebrating, to celebrate while progressing" finally appeared from the nimbus of *brevitas romana*, "Roman brevity," illustrated by Caesar: *Veni, vidi, vici*, ("I came, I saw, I conquered.") Born in Roman soil, the prayers carried the glorious mark of their origin: sobriety, dignity, gravity. The reform also wanted the rites "to be remarkable by their brevity."[17] That is what our prayers are indeed.

Although they are theologically perfect, liturgically correct, and literally cannot be criticized, our prayers translated into English do not arouse enthusiasm. No one criticizes them. But no one admires them. The translation of a dead language, even adorned with the splendor of the past, does not necessarily create a living text suited to our time. The invocation *Omnipotens sempiterne Deus*, "Almighty and eternal God," used to evoke among the ancients the royal majesty and infinite almightiness of God (as he appears in the paintings that decorate the apses of our Roman churches, with immense eyes that scrutinize the universe). But who invokes God today as the Almighty? Therefore, it is with reason that the majority of linguistic groups write—or have already written—new prayers which are not translations of ancient texts.

The community ratifies the presidential prayer with the acclamation *Amen*.

Amen is the transcription of a Hebrew word whose root evokes that which is solid, stable, true, and faithful. The Hebrew word can be used as an adjective or as an adverb. Isaiah 65:16 speaks about God-amen (the Greek translates: the true God), that is, the God on whom one can rely in all confidence, the God for every faithful. As an adverb, *Amen* means either *It is so* (Luke ordinarily trans-

---

[17] *Constitution on the Sacred Liturgy (Sacrosanctum Concilium)*, 34.

lates it as *alēthōs*, "truly"), or *May it be so* (*genoito*, "May that happen").

The liturgy uses the adverb *Amen* in these two meanings. When we affirm: "God [is] maker of heaven and earth" (as in the Creed) or further: "His marvelous love fills the universe" (as in Ps 33:5), the response is not: "May it be so." Because it is that way whether we recognize it or not. We can simply respond: Truly, it is so. That is the meaning of the *Amen* that follows all the doxologies. But when we implore God: "Have mercy on us and forgive us our sins," we humbly add: "*Amen*, may it be so!"

In the New Testament, *Amen* is the personal name of Jesus. John writes in the Book of Revelation: "Thus speaks the *Amen*, the faithful and true witness" (Rev 3:14). By ratifying the prayers and the doxology that ends the anaphora with *Amen*, the faithful remember that they are pronouncing at the same time the name of Jesus. They ask for the fulfillment of the promise of their Lord: "Whatever you ask the Father in my name will be granted to you" (John 15:16). For they know that when their prayer rises to the throne of God, it is welcomed by the Risen One, "always living to intercede in their favor" (Heb 7:25).

Part Two
Liturgy of the Word

Vatican II had asked that the biblical treasures be opened more fully for the faithful.[1] To implement these reforms a "Consilium" went to work in 1965 at the end of the Council. The official edition of the new Lectionary appeared May 25, 1969. The Christian community welcomed it on the First Sunday of Advent, November 30, 1969. The oldest Lectionary of the Roman Church, containing Epistles and Gospels, dates from the seventh century.[2] Thus the new Lectionary replaces a book which had served the community for twelve centuries. That shows its importance and its newness.

Structure of the Lectionary

Let us recall the structure of the Sunday Lectionary for Ordinary Time.

The First Reading is taken from the Old Testament. It is chosen in relationship to the Gospel. It illustrates what tradition liked to call the ecclesial symphony of the two choirs of the Old and New Testaments. The Responsorial Psalm is the community's response to that reading.

The Second Reading presents the Letters of the New Testament. It is "continuous" (or more exactly, semi-continuous), spread out

---

[1] *Constitution on the Sacred Liturgy (Sacrosanctum Concilium)*, 51.

[2] According to J. A. Jungmann, *Missarum Solemnia*, vol. 1 (1956), Aubier, Coll. Théologie, 37, p. 94.

in a three-year cycle. The Gospel, which is also semi-continuous, is likewise read over a three-year cycle.

Here, for example, is how this schema works for the Thirty-First Sunday in Ordinary Time, Cycle B:

> *First Reading* (non-continuous)
> Deuteronomy 6:2-6: "You shall love the Lord your God with all your heart . . ."
>
> *Responsorial Psalm*
> Psalm 17: "I love you, Lord, my strength."
>
> *Second Reading* (semi-continuous)
> Letter to the Hebrews 7:23-28
> (Reading of the preceding Sunday: Heb 5:1-6
> Reading of the following Sunday: Heb 9:24-28)
>
> *Third Reading* (semi-continuous)
> Gospel according to Mark 12:28-34: The commandment
>   of love: "You shall love the Lord your God"
> (Reading of the preceding Sunday: Mark 10:46-52
> Reading of the following Sunday: Mark 12:38-44)

Let us note that the synagogal service, which included the reading of the Law and the Prophets followed by a homily (Acts 13:5), spread the readings over a three-year cycle according to Palestinian tradition.[3] By spreading the Gospels over three years, the Lectionary is inspired by a practice that is two thousand years old.

Ministerial Function of the Celebration of the Word

What is the ministerial function of the biblical readings? Why read the Bible when we celebrate the Eucharist? No more were we baptized in order to sing, as mentioned previously, were we baptized to read the Bible, but to enter into a Covenant with God.

The oldest celebration of the Word according to the Bible coincides precisely with the first celebration of the Covenant of Sinai according to Exod 24:1-11. Tradition has blended the Priestly and

---

[3] See L. Deiss, *God's Word and God's People* (Collegeville, Minn.: The Liturgical Press, 1974), pp. 97–115.

Yahwist sources of these accounts, and we can no longer reconstruct the historic event. Yet, we perceive perfectly the teaching of tradition.[4]

First, there is a proclamation of the Word: Moses took the Book of the Covenant and read it aloud to the people who declared: "Everything that Yahweh has said, we will put into practice, and we will obey" (Exod 24:7).

Then, there is the sacrifice of the Covenant: Moses took the blood (of the victims that had been immolated), sprinkled it over the people and said: "This is the blood of the Covenant that Yahweh has made with you in accordance with all these words" (Exod 24:8).

Finally, there is the communion meal: Moses went up, accompanied by seventy elders of Israel. They saw the God of Israel . . . They ate and they drank (Exod 24:9-11).

This structure is exactly the one of the Mass today. First, there is the proclamation of God's Word. Then, there is the sacrifice when the priest, at the consecration, repeats the words of Moses: "This is the blood of the Covenant." Finally, there is the "meal" of communion in the reception of the Eucharist.

Vatican II spoke about the "extreme importance" of God's Word.[5] This extreme importance is the very one of the Eucharist. Summing up the teaching of tradition, the Council affirms: "The Church has always venerated the divine Scriptures as she venerated the Body of the Lord, in so far as she never ceases, particularly in the sacred Liturgy, to partake of the bread of life and to offer it to the faithful from the one table of the Word of God and the Body of Christ."[6] That is why the Magisterium could rightly speak about the "real presence" of Christ in the Word.[7] If it is necessary to distinguish "the two parts which in a sense go to make up

---

[4] *Ibid.*, pp. 3-39 and 253-264. The Yahwist source is the name given to the biblical tradition which dates from 950 B.C. in which God is called Yahweh. The Elohist source is the biblical tradition which dates from the ninth-eighth centuries B.C. in which God is most frequently called Elohim. The final text as it appears in the Bible is the result of an edited work which used these sources.

[5] *Constitution on the Sacred Liturgy (Sacrosanctum Concilium)*, 24.

[6] *Constitution on Divine Revelation (Dei Verbum)*, 21.

[7] Instruction *Eucharisticum Mysterium* (May 25, 1967), 1E.

the Mass, that is, the Liturgy of the Word and the Liturgy of the Eucharist," it must be added immediately that these two parts "are so closely joined that they constitute a single act of worship."[8] And this single act of worship is the celebration of the Covenant.

This is a marvelous teaching that, after centuries of forgetfulness or carelessness, restores the Word to the place that tradition assigned it. Saint Jerome (†419/420) affirmed: "I think that the Gospel is the body of Christ and that the Holy Scriptures are his doctrine. When the Lord speaks about eating his flesh and drinking his blood certainly this can mean the mystery (of the Eucharist). However, his true body and blood are (also) the Word of the Scriptures and its doctrine."[9]

The Responsorial Psalm: Canticle of the Covenant

God speaks to the people by doing marvels for them. The people respond by celebrating those marvels. Thus God leads the people of the Exodus across the Red Sea. Miriam, the tambourine player, celebrates the Lord who threw horse and rider into the sea (Exod 15 and 21). God delivers Hannah from her barrenness by giving her little Samuel. Hannah responds by celebrating the Lord who enables a barren woman to give birth seven times (1 Sam 2:5). God delivers Tobit from his blindness. Tobit responds by praising the Lord who lets God's light shine on Jerusalem at the same time as in the heart of Tobit (Tob 13:11). In the New Testament God blesses the virginity of Mary by making her the mother of Jesus. Mary glorifies the Lord; she exults in God her *Savior* and in this *Jesus* that she carries within her.

This is precisely the ministerial function of the Responsorial Psalm in the liturgical celebration. In fact, the Word commemorates old marvels, the community celebrates those deeds today and actualizes them on the level of its celebration: it *responds* to the God of marvels through the *Responsorial* Psalm. We will notice the structure of the dialogue that the Lectionary establishes between the Word that comes from God and the word that comes from the community:

---

[8] *Constitution on the Sacred Liturgy (Sacrosanctum Concilium)*, 56.
[9] *In Isaiam, Prologus (Corpus Christianorum), Ser. Lat., vol. 63*, p. 1.

Word of God: Old Testament.
—*The community responds:* Psalm.
Word of God: Letters from the New Testament.
—*The community sings:* Acclamation to the Gospel.
Word of God: Gospel.
—*The community prays:* Prayer of the Faithful.

We used to say that the Word proclaimed is the word of the Covenant. The Psalm that responds to it is the canticle of the Covenant. The Word prepares for the Covenant, making us enter into it. The Psalm sings its grace, imploring God to keep us in it.

No more than we can replace the Gospel with a simply human word, beautiful as it may be, or replace the Eucharistic bread with ordinary bread, can we replace the Responsorial Psalm with a simply human canticle, marvelous as it may be. That would be to defraud in the service of God, or, as Paul says, "to trade on the Word of God" (2 Cor 2:17). Instead of recognizing the face of Christ in the Psalm of the Covenant, the community would only recognize a human face.

In his last appearance to his apostles right before his Ascension, Jesus speaks to them about what is written concerning him in "the Law, the Prophets, and the Psalms" (Luke 24:44). Therefore the story of Jesus is found in the Psalms. Every Sunday, the community is invited to read a page of that story, to discover an aspect of the face of Jesus. After long centuries during which that blessed face was hidden—sometimes even by the splendor of the neumes of the Gregorian chant, which, while wanting to magnify it, actually hid it in the dazzle of melodies—this face appears once again to the community in its marvelous beauty. May the community recognize it!

The Alleluia and the Gospel Procession

Alleluia is the transcription of the Hebrew *Halelu-Yah*, which means Praise-Yah (=Yahweh). Therefore is it a matter of an invitation to praise. We encounter it at the beginning and at the end of Pss 146–150. It is also found as a song of the angels in the heavenly liturgy of the Revelation (19:1, 3, 4, 6). It is the second time—after the *Gloria*—that the earthly liturgy borrows its song from the angels. They will return once again in the singing of the *Sanctus*. Our earthly liturgy, open to heaven, is inhabited by angels. Even the smallest community is surrounded by angelic multitudes.

The ministerial function of the Alleluia—or of the song that replaces it during Lent—is to accompany the procession of the Gospel Book.[10]

The order of this rite in its simplest form is presented in this way: the priest takes the Gospel Book, the Word of Christ, from the altar, which represents Christ, and he carries it to the lectern, the place of the Word of God. For the correct fulfillment of the ministerial function of this procession of the Gospel Book, several points are to be considered.

The Gospel Book

Tradition, wisdom of the past, teaches us that from the fifth-sixth century, Christian veneration surrounded with honor the book which contained the Gospels. Some were written in gold on parchment of gold. The covers were sometimes extravagantly sumptuous. On an Evangeliary (Gospel Book) of the tenth-eleventh century offered by Charles V in 1379 and preserved at the Sainte- Chapelle, 104 pearls, 35 sapphires, 24 rubies, and 30 emeralds sparkle. In the Byzantine churches, the Evangeliary is ordinarily the richest treasure. To be sure, it is not a question of copying the riches of the past but by imitating its spirit. The *Lectionary for Mass* states with lyricism: "The proclamation of the gospel always stands as the high point of the liturgy of the word. Thus the liturgical traditions of both the East and the West have consistently continued to preserve some distinction between the books for readings. The Book of the Gospels was always designed with the utmost care and was more ornate and shown greater respect than any of the other books of readings. In our times also, then, it is very desirable that cathedrals and at least the larger, more populous parishes and the churches with a larger attendance possess a beautifully designed Book of the Gospels, separate from the other book of readings."[11] The Lection-

---

[10] *General Instruction of the Roman Missal*, 94 and 131.
[11] *Lectionary for Mass*, 36.

ary is surely an optimistic book which sees the future filled with liturgical splendors.

The Exposition of the Gospel Book on the Altar

The Missal provides for the placement of the Gospel Book on the altar either at the beginning of the Mass or before the proclamation of the Gospel.[12] This placement is practically equal to an "enthronement." We know that at the time of the celebration of the Councils, the Gospel Book was solemnly enthroned. Cyril of Alexandria (†444) reports that at the time of the Council at Ephesus in 431, "the holy Synod, assembled at the Church dedicated to Mary, instituted Christ in some way as member and head of the Council. In fact, the venerable Gospel was placed on a throne."[13] Vatican II splendidly restored this rite of enthronement.

The Showing of the Evangeliary

The priest, standing in the middle before the altar, lifts up the Gospel book (Evangeliary) and shows it (to the people), signifying through it the manifestation of the Savior when He began to show himself to the crowds.

The Hagios (the "Sanctus"), repeated three times, is the acclamation of the angels . . . "We sing this hymn after the presentation and the entrance of the Gospel as to proclaim that in coming among us Christ placed us and established us in the choirs of angels."

Nicholas Cabasilas (fourteenth century),
A Commentary on the Divine Liturgy, 20.
SC 4 bis (1967), pp. 147, 148.
tr. J.M. Hussey and P.A. McNulty (London: SPCK, 1960).

Until the ninth and tenth centuries, only the Gospel Book and the Eucharist enjoyed the privilege of being placed on the altar, the

---

[12] *General Instruction of the Roman Missal, 79.*
[13] *Apologeticus ad Theodosium Imp.*—PG 76,472 CD.

symbol of Christ. It would be good to go back to the ancient tradition and remove from the altar the objects that do not strictly have any purpose there, such as the cruets of water and wine, with the bowl for washing hands and the hand towel, not forgetting the plastic under the bowl . . . When one is invited to dinner, one does not wash one's hands at the family table. Why, then, do some priests wash their hands at "the Lord's table"? (1 Cor 10:21) In the same way, one does not place towels on the table. Why, then, should the hand towel lie on the altar? Nor does one place one's hat on the table. Why do some bishops—may God forgive them—place their skullcaps on it? I wish to heaven that these remarks were unnecessary!

The Procession

Among the processions that take place in the course of the Mass, the procession of the Gospel should be the most festive and the most joyous.

The ancient Ordo of the Gallican liturgy (sixth century) explains: "Just as the procession of the Holy Gospel goes forward, so too the power of Christ triumphs over death, in the midst of songs and seven candles . . . The deacon goes up to the pulpit, just like Christ goes to the seat of the Father, and from there he proclaims the gifts of life while the clergy proclaim: Glory to you, O Lord!" And after the proclamation of the Gospel, according to the same Ordo, the clergy sing the *Sanctus*, just like the saints of the heavenly liturgy of the Revelation who sing to celebrate the risen Christ.[14]

The new Order of Mass, which is much less expansive, does credit to the *sobrietas romana*. It simply provides that the deacon or priest "may be accompanied by ministers with incense and candles." However, it keeps the essential of the rite, the procession of the Gospel Book,[15] to signify the essential of our faith, the veneration and praise of Christ, the Word of God.

Numerous communities throughout the world have enriched the *sobrietas romana* by surrounding the procession of the Gospel with

---

[14] K. Gamber, *Ordo Antiquus Gallicanus*, Regensburg: Pustet, 1965, p. 18.
[15] See *General Instruction of the Roman Missal*, 79 and 131.

flowers, candles and dances. We do not live only on the bread of the Gospel clearly proclaimed, but also on joy and beauty. Progressively, joy is invading our celebrations. By dancing for the Lord, these communities fulfill the will of God who said through his Holy Spirit: "Praise God with dancing!" (Ps 150:4).

The Lectern (Ambo)

The past had created places of splendor from which to proclaim the Word. Some pulpits of our cathedrals are true jewels of stone. The pulpit of San Agnello of the sixth century at Ravenna (Italy) measures almost six meters long and three meters high! The pulpit of Hagia Sophia in Constantinople (rebuilt after the earthquake of 558) is from the same period. It is said that "its tremendous mass made it resemble a tower shining with the fires of innumerable precious stones encased in marbles of the rarest and most striking colors."[16]

Let us make allowances for Eastern hyperbole. Let us also pass over the richness that has never been synonymous with beauty. But we can be in full agreement with what the General Instruction provides: "The dignity of the word of God requires the church to have a place that is suitable for proclamation of the word. . . . As a rule the lectern or ambo should be stationary, not simply a movable stand. . . . The readings, responsorial psalm, and the Easter Proclamation (*Exsultet*) are proclaimed from the lectern; it may be used also for the homily and general intercessions (prayer of the faithful). It is better for the commentator, cantor, or choir director not to use the lectern."[17]

Those are words of wisdom. The lectern is the place for God's Word, not for human words.

The Lectionary for Mass adds: "Great pains must therefore be taken, in keeping with the design of each church, over the harmonious and close relationship of the lectern with the altar."[18] In a word, the theology of two tables, the table of the Word and the table of the Eucharist, must not be expressed only on the intellectual level, but also on the level of the architecture.

[16] Paul le Silentiaire, *Descriptio ambonis.*—PG 86, 2251-2264. Cited by H. Leclercq, art. "Ambon" in DACL, vol. 1, col. 1333.

[17] *General Instruction of the Roman Missal*, 272.

[18] *Lectionary for Mass*, 32.

Much has already been done. We have taken away the shabby stands which, the day after the Council, were quite astonished at having been enthroned in the sanctuaries and at being treated like pulpits. We have also taken away the pulpits of useless majesty behind which the reader disappeared just leaving his head to emerge between two wings of an eagle. But the field remains open. One dreams of simple and majestic lecterns, true monstrances for the Word of God, in harmony with the altar.

The Proclamation of the Gospel

The proclamation of the Gospel is considered as the summit of the celebration of the Word. Of course the First Reading, from the Old Testament, the Responsorial Psalm, as well as the readings from the Pauline Corpus or other New Testament texts all have the same dignity as the reading from the Gospel. Saint Irenaeus said: "The writings of Moses are the words of Christ."[19] But it is here, in the reading from the Gospel, that the teaching of the Council is realized with the most visibility: "It is Christ who speaks when the Holy Scriptures are read in the Church."[20] The words of Jesus crown the words of the prophets: "After having spoken to our forefathers through the prophets at many times and in many ways in the past, God speaks to us in these last days through his Son" (Heb 1:1-2).

Another aspect of the mystery of the Word is glaringly affirmed here. The reading of the Word of God has never been, neither in the synagogal liturgy nor in the Christian liturgy, a simple reading as would be the reading of the archives of the People of God of the Old and New Testaments. Of course, by familiarizing us with the past of the Church, such a reading is highly enriching. But the reading of the Gospel is rather a celebration of Christ. Actually, it is he whom we acclaim and not the book when we say at the beginning of the reading of the Gospel: "Glory to you, Lord," and at the end: "Praise to you, Lord Jesus Christ." In the eighth century, all the clergy venerated the Gospel Book by kissing it. In

---

[19] *Against Heresies*, IV, 2,3.
[20] *Constitution on the Sacred Liturgy (Sacrosanctum Concilium)*, 7.

some communities (Coptic and Ethiopian), the entire community kisses the book as it does the cross of Christ on Good Friday.

The Missal sums up the tradition: "The liturgy itself inculcates the great reverence to be shown toward the reading of the gospel."[21] And this veneration is the one that is given to Christ.

The Homily

In its simplest form, the homily is the translation and explanation of the Word of God. The most typical example with regard to this is the homily given by Ezra, priest and scribe, to the deported who were returning from Babylonian captivity. This took place around the year 400 at the time of a solemn celebration of the Law at the Feast of Tents in Jerusalem. "All the people assembled as one man in the square before the Water Gate . . . Ezra read from the Book of the Law of God, translating and giving the meaning. Thus the people understood the reading" (Neh 8:1, 8). Ezra read the original Hebrew text, a language that had become archaic among the people, especially since the deportation. The Levites translated it into Aramaic, the dominant language in Assyria-Babylonia, which had become the usual language of the Zionists.

In its highest form, the homily is the actualization of God's Word on the level of the celebrating community. The most typical example here is the homily of Jesus at the synagogue of Nazareth. After the reading from the Book of Isaiah, Jesus begins his homily with these words: "Today is fulfilled this word that you have just heard" (Luke 4:21).

In spite of the four centuries that separate them, these two homilies are joined in the sense that the goal of the homily will always be to translate the Word of God by showing its actuality.

The Homily: Word of God

The Greek *homilia* means reunion, company, or familiar conversation. The homily shares in the very mystery of Jesus. He ap-

---

[21] *General Instruction of the Roman Missal*, 35.

peared like an ordinary man, but he was at the same time the Son of God. The homily appears like familiar conversation, but it is at the same time Word of God. Of course, it does not possess the universal value possessed by the Bible, which, according to the canon of Scriptures, the Church recognizes as the authentic Word of God. But it is God's word on the level of the celebrating community. The golden rule for the speaker is the following: "If someone speaks, let it be as words of God" (1 Pet 4:11). The golden rule for listeners is to receive these words as words of God. Paul said to his Thessalonians: "You have welcomed the word not as a human word, but as what it really is, the Word of God" (1 Thess 2:13). Just as only the Spirit of God can transform the bread of the earth into bread of heaven, thus only the grace of the Holy Spirit can transfigure familiar human words into true words of God. The principle of ancient exegesis formulated by Gregory the Wonder-Worker (†circa 270) is valid for both the speaker and the listener: "The same grace is needed for those who pronounce the prophecy (that is, the divine Word) as for those who hear it. And no one can understand the prophecy if the Spirit who prophesied does not grant him the understanding of his words."[22]

A Biblical Church

The diffusion of Bibles among Christian people has occurred in our time at a level never attained in preceding ages. And yet, for the immense majority of the faithful, it is really the Lectionary that constitutes their only Bible; the readings of the Mass, their only biblical readings; and the homily, their only explanation and actualization of God's Word. This must be added: because of minimalism of Sunday—only one Mass per week—the faithful, and further, only the churchgoers, are in contact with the Word of God only once a week. This underlines the importance of the homily.

In this renewal desired by Vatican II to transform the heavy ecclesial institution into a biblical Church—not a Church of biblicists whose principal concern would be exegesis, but a Church rooted

---

[22] *Thanksgiving to Origen,* XV, 179.

in the Word—the homily is a "compulsory passage." The renewal of our communities depends in part on the quality of our homilies.

Of course, this perfecting of the homily concerns those who have accepted the ministry of speaking in the name of God. In a certain sense, one can even say that each baptized person has accepted to speak about God if only through the example of his or her life: every Christian is a word of God for his or her brothers and sisters. This renewal of the homily also concerns all those who listen to the Word, therefore, the entire Christian community. For there is a threshold in the conscience of every baptized person that no preacher can cross, the threshold where the noise of human words dies and where each one must say again with little Samuel: "Speak, Lord, your servant is listening" (1 Sam 3:11). No one can give this irreplaceable homily in our place. It is heard in silence and adoration and actualized in the love of obedience.

The Profession of Faith

The profession of faith, "serves as a way for the people to respond and to give their assent to the word of God heard in the readings and through the homily and for them to call to mind the truths of faith before they begin to celebrate the eucharist."[23]

According to the popular sensibility, the Creed, especially if it is chanted in Latin in great gatherings, has great emotional and symbolic value. It is the affirmation of the oneness of the faith not only across diverse communities but also across the ages.

If faith is essential in the celebration of the Eucharist, rightly called "mystery of faith," the recitation or singing of the Creed is, in return, rather secondary in that celebration. It is an element similar to those statues in cathedrals that can be moved or even taken away without endangering the solidity of the edifice. That is really what happens since the majority of the Masses do not have the Creed, and the equilibrium of the celebration is not threatened because of that, but rather improved. We affirm easily, and we sing willingly that Jesus "was begotten, not made, of the same substance as the Father" (Creed from Nicaea-Constantinople); but, for example, the

[23] *General Instruction of the Roman Missal*, 43.

Roman liturgy used three forms of the Creed: the symbol of the
Apostles, the symbol of Saint Athanasius (which was taken away
from the Divine Office in 1955), and the symbol of Nicaea-
Constantinople, which adds to the symbol of the Apostles the affirmations of the Councils of Nicaea (325) and Constantinople (381).

The Creed was inserted into the Mass slowly. The formulas of
Nicaea-Constantinople served as roadblocks for Christological errors. In Rome, the Creed was introduced into the Mass at the beginning of the eleventh century. When the emperor Henry came
to Rome in 1014, he put pressure on Pope Benedict VIII to adopt
in the papal city the custom of the Creed which was in use in the
imperial court.[24]

The Creed raises several questions. One can wonder if the formulas of Nicaea-Constantinople, marked by the Christological quar-
rels of the fourth century, are the most apt to express the Christian
faith today. Are we ready to declare today that we are combating
the "structures of sin" which exist in the world and which oppress
the poor?[25] Do we believe that the richest nations must come to
the aid of the poorest nations? That, however, is the teaching of
the encyclical *Sollicitudo rei socialis* (December 30, 1987) and this
teaching is deeply rooted in the Gospel. Such affirmations would
engage us more than the affirmation that the Son is consubstantial
to the Father. On the other hand, numerous professions of faith
exist in the New Testament. They have the incomparable dignity
of God's Word. If the words and the errors that they combat whirl
about in the wind of history, only the Word of God "stands eter-
nally" (Isa 40:8). Finally, let us note that the best profession of faith
is the actual celebration of the Eucharist. Besides, the Eucharistic
Prayers II and IV propose excellent formulas of the Creed centered
not on theological discussions but on the history of salvation through
Jesus Christ.

This having been said, one must not take bread away from the
mouths of children: if a community delights in singing the Creed
in Latin, why not let it satisfy itself with this bread, especially if

---

[24] J. A. Jungmann, *op. cit.*, vol. 2, p. 242.
[25] Encyclical *Sollicitudo rei socialis*, 36.

it is engaged at the same time in living according to the Gospel, which is the best profession of faith?

The Prayer of the Faithful

The restoration of the Prayer of the Faithful is surely one of the best successes of the liturgical reform. The General Instruction presents it in this way: "In the general intercessions or prayer of the faithful, the people, exercising their priestly function, intercede for all humanity. . . . As a rule the sequence of intentions is to be: a) for the needs of the Church; b) for public authorities and the salvation of the world; c) for those oppressed by any need; d) for the local community."[26]

This prayer is a direct legacy of the Jewish tradition which liked to add prayers of request to its benedictions.[27] It acquired such favor that it was repeated excessively. Thus the *Apostolic Constitutions* (circa 380) present, before the Eucharistic Prayer, a litany for the catechumens and another for the faithful, and after the Eucharistic Prayer, a third said by the bishop and a fourth said by the deacon.[28] The multiplication of these litanies brought about a certain devaluation of the esteem people had for them.

Prayer of the Faithful and Kyrie

In Rome, the Prayer of the Faithful disappeared from the Mass towards the sixth century. That is the same time that the *Kyrie* appeared at the beginning of the Mass. But we have not yet been able to specify what the relationship was between these two forms of litany. The mist of history has not yet dissipated from the horizon of these prayers.

By restoring both the Prayer of the Faithful and the *Kyrie* under the form of a litany, Vatican II put an end to fourteen centuries of liturgical nonchalance.

---

[26] *General Instruction of the Roman Missal*, 45–46.
[27] See L. Deiss, *Springtime of the Liturgy* (Collegeville, Minn.: The Liturgical Press, 1979), pp. 3–19; the prayer of the *Eighteen Blessings* or the blessing which accompanies the *Shema Israel*.
[28] *Ibid.*, pp. 191–193 and 197–198.

Prayer of the Faithful and Word of God

After the Consecration, there is another series of intercessions for the Pope, the bishops, the priests, the deceased, and all the people of God.

So that these intercessions do not form a doublet with the Prayer of the Faithful, it is good that the latter be enriched and illuminated by the Word that has just been proclaimed. The Order of Mass says very well: "Having been fed by this word [the people] make their

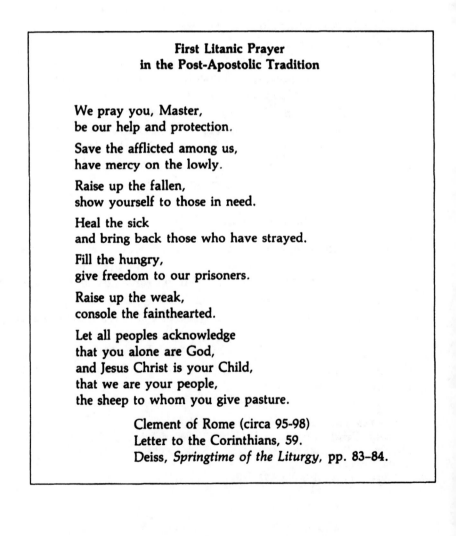

**First Litanic Prayer
in the Post-Apostolic Tradition**

We pray you, Master,
be our help and protection.

Save the afflicted among us,
have mercy on the lowly.

Raise up the fallen,
show yourself to those in need.

Heal the sick
and bring back those who have strayed.

Fill the hungry,
give freedom to our prisoners.

Raise up the weak,
console the fainthearted.

Let all peoples acknowledge
that you alone are God,
and Jesus Christ is your Child,
that we are your people,
the sheep to whom you give pasture.

Clement of Rome (circa 95-98)
Letter to the Corinthians, 59.
Deiss, *Springtime of the Liturgy*, pp. 83–84.

petitions in the general intercessions for the needs of the Church and for the salvation of the whole world."[29]

Prayer of the Faithful, Mystery of Love

Vatican II affirms that each particular church must "represent the Universal Church as perfectly as possible."[30] As a sign of the universal Church, each community must also be a sign of its universal prayer. Therefore, the future of the Church and of humanity rests on each community, including the smallest and most humble: each community intercedes before God for several billions of people.

This Prayer of the Faithful is called universal not because it presents to the Lord all the intentions of all the members of the celebrating community, but first because all the members intercede for the needs of all the people in the world. Therefore, it is not limited to the presentation to God of the mischief and fighting of all its members: it is the catholic, that is, universal prayer of the priestly people for the universe. Between God and the nations of the world, God has placed each Christian community, little as it may be. Between God and the pain of humanity, God has placed the intercession of the smallest community. The Prayer of the Faithful is the mystery of love that binds this community to the universe.

It joins in this way the mystery of the Eucharist. Indeed, just as the blood of Christ is poured out not only for the salvation of the celebrating community but for the salvation of all of humanity, thus the Prayer of the Faithful likewise intercedes for all of humanity.

Of course, particular and personal intentions are not forgotten. They are much more welcomed by God when they are integrated into the Prayer of the Faithful

We know that God's ear is sharp, so sharp that in the most general intentions God discerns each voice that cries out, that in the immense clamor of humanity that rises to the divine throne, God discerns the most humble plea, from those who hardly dare to murmur their sadness, to those who hide their faces. When "the afflicted

---

[29] *General Instruction of the Roman Missal*, 33.
[30] *Decree on the Church's Missionary Activity (Ad Gentes)*, 20.

person cried out, God heard" (Ps 34:7). Such is the principle of the Prayer of the Faithful.

In the celebration of the Word, the community presents its face to God and allows the features of the divine message to be drawn there, as in a mirror. In the Prayer of the Faithful, it presents to God this face marked by the Word. In the time of Isaiah, when King Hezekiah received a letter from Sennacherib telling him that the Assyrians were going to burn Jerusalem and put the inhabitants to the sword, he went up to the Temple, unfolded the letter before Yahweh and said: "Yahweh, open your eyes and see!" (2 Kgs 19:16). In the Prayer of the Faithful the community presents its face fashioned by the Word, and likewise says to God: "Lord, open your eyes and see!"

Conclusion: the Task

In 1973, when he was 80 years old, Father B. Botte, who was a great crafter of the liturgical reform, wrote: "Imagine that the Church would make an abrupt change, after which she would become a community of saints. This is a dangerous illusion. It is enough to reread the parable of the tares to be convinced. But there is another parable that gives me hope; it is the one of the sower. I believe in the power of the Word of God . . . There is a great deal of good earth eager to open itself to the seed of God's Word. It only needs to be given to it. That is what the Council asks: an inspired preaching of the Word of God which enlightens and nourishes the faith of the faithful. In my opinion, that is the greatest problem of liturgical reform."[31]

Those are words of wisdom.

---

[31] B. Botte, *Le mouvement liturgique* (Paris: Desclée et Cie, 1973), pp. 207–208.

Part Three
Eucharistic Liturgy

At the time of the celebration of the Last Supper, Jesus took bread and wine, pronounced the prayer of thanksgiving, and then distributed the bread and the wine to his disciples. The Eucharistic liturgy follows the rhythm of the celebration of the Last Supper. Therefore three parts are distinguished in it: the bringing of the bread and the wine, the prayer of thanksgiving, and, finally, the distribution of Communion. The Order of the Mass notes:

1. "In the preparation of the gifts, the bread and the wine with water are brought to the altar, that is, the same elements that Christ used.

2. In the eucharistic prayer, thanks is given to God for the whole work of salvation and the gifts of bread and wine become the body and blood of Christ.

3. . . . through communion [the faithful] receive the Lord's body and blood in the same way the apostles received them from Christ's own hands."[1]

1. THE PREPARATION OF THE GIFTS

The old Offertory resembled a magnificent garden in which tradition, through the ages, had planted the most marvelous flowers,

[1] *General Instruction of the Roman Missal*, 48.

but outside of the flowerbeds; everything was in bloom, but almost nothing was in place.

When presenting the gifts, one said a fervent prayer of offering (*Suscipe, sancte Pater*), in which one beseeched God to welcome this "immaculate host," which was still only bread. A prayer of forgiveness for "the innumerable sins, offenses, and negligences" was also added. Then one offered "the chalice of salvation for the salvation of the entire world" (*Offerimus tibi*). But this chalice still contained only wine and water.

There was also an epiclesis (*Veni, sanctificator*), in which one asked the Holy Spirit to bless this sacrifice, whereas the epiclesis traditionally surrounded the account of the Institution.

There was even a prayer of offering addressed to the Trinity (*Suscipe, sancta Trinitas*), whereas, according to the Council of Hippo in 393, ancient tradition asked that "at the altar, the prayer must always be addressed to the Father."[2] This prayer also presented a mini-anamnesis: it recalled "the passion, resurrection, and ascension of our Lord Jesus Christ," which characterizes the anamnesis at the heart of the Eucharistic prayer. Finally, it asks "the blessed ever-virgin Mary, blessed John the Baptist, the holy apostles, and all the saints" to intercede for us in heaven.

There was a new prayer of purification in the *Lavabo:* it was added to the prayer of forgiveness of the *Suscipe, sancte Pater.*

Realizing that he was praying all alone, the priest would turn toward the assembly, ask for its help, adding that his sacrifice was also theirs. That was the *Orate, fratres.*

All these prayers, which were as beautiful as bouquets, had ended up disfiguring the garden of the offertory. The reform cleaned the flowerbeds and walks. It did it with boldness and timidity. The boldness is manifested when it changed the very name from the *Offertory* to the "*Preparation of the Gifts.*" Therefore it was no longer a matter of offering and encroaching on the Eucharistic Prayer. The timidity is revealed when it kept, nevertheless, the word "offertory"[3] (as in the mention of the song of the offertory). Accustomed to the old offertory, those who prepared the new prayers

---

[2] J. A. Jungmann, *Missarum Solemnia*, vol. 2, p. 140.
[3] *General Instruction of the Roman Missal*, 50 (Appendix, 4th ed., 1975).

for the "Preparation of the Gifts" kept in their hearts, like a scar, the memory of the ancient prayers.

The Bringing of the Bread

The General Instruction recommends that "it is desirable for the faithful to present the bread and wine. . . . Even though the faithful no longer, as in the past, bring the bread and wine for the liturgy from their homes, the rite of carrying up the gifts retains the same spiritual value and meaning."[4]

Thus the Missal renews relations with the oldest tradition. In the first description of the Mass (circa 150), Justin notes that after the Prayers and the Kiss of Peace, "one brought bread and a cup of wine to the one who presided over the assembly of the faithful."[5] This custom was dear to Christian piety. The people recognized in the practice the exercise of their royal priesthood. Hippolytus (†circa 235) notes that the catechumens bring what is necessary for the Eucharist of their baptismal Mass because they have become worthy of it.[6] Augustine (354-430) relates that his mother, Monica, "did not let a day go by without bringing her offering to the altar."[7]

At the Last Supper, Jesus had used unleavened bread, according to the Passover ritual. The Christian community which celebrated the Lord's Supper not once a year—like the feast of Passover—but every Sunday and even during the week, quite naturally used homemade bread. This bread sometimes had the form of a crown, like a round braid, or even the form of a round bread. It was only toward the ninth century that unleavened bread was progressively substituted for ordinary bread. This practice will finally become imperative in the eleventh century. The round hosts that we know appeared towards the twelfth century when they were cut in unleavened dough *"in modum denarii,"* in the form of coins.[8] The use of these wafers of bread stopped the baking of the Eucharistic bread by the faithful and its presentation at the altar by the con-

---

[4] *General Instruction of the Roman Missal,* 49.
[5] *Apology,* 1,65.
[6] *Apostolic Tradition,* 20.
[7] *Confessions,* V, 9, 17.
[8] J. A. Jungmann, *op. cit.,* vol. 2, p. 30.

Jewish Blessings

The Kiddush
for the Sabbath and Feast Days

The word *kiddush* means "sanctification" and it is the name of the blessing pronounced at the beginning of each Sabbath and feast day, at the moment when the first stars appear and the Sabbath lamp has been lit. It separates profane time from time which is more specially consecrated to God.

The prayer comprises a blessing over the wine, a blessing of the day, and a blessing over the bread. These blessings are said at the table by the father of the family, with his family and guests around him.

Blessing for the Wine

Blessed are you, Lord our God,
King of the universe,
you who created the fruit of the vine.

Blessing for the Feast

Blessed are you, Lord our God,
King of the universe.
You have sanctified us by your commandments,
you have given us as an inheritance the Sabbath of your holiness
out of love and good will,
as a memorial of the works of your creation (Lev 23:3).
This day is the first of your holy convocations.
It is the memorial of the exodus from Egypt.
You have chosen us among all the peoples.
You have sanctified us.
You have given us as an inheritance the Sabbath of your holiness
out of love and good will.
Blessed are you, O Lord, who sanctifies the Sabbath!

Blessing for the Bread

Blessed are you, Lord our God,
King of the universe, you who have brought bread forth from the
earth.

Springtime of the Liturgy, pp. 5–6.

---

gregation. When there are many people receiving communion, these
hosts are very convenient. In other cases, the use of a flatcake of
bread is preferable. The General Instruction quite rightly notes that
"the nature of the sign demands that the material for the eucharistic celebration truly have the appearance of food."[9]

The prayer that accompanies the presentation of the bread is
noteworthy for its antiquity and noble beauty:

> Blessed are you, Lord, God of all creation.
> Through your goodness we have this bread to offer,
> which earth has given and human hands have made.
> It will become for us the bread of life.

This prayer is in fact inspired directly by the Jewish blessing that
the father of the family said over the bread at the beginning of the
meal. Therefore, it was recited by Jesus at the Last Supper. In returning to it, the priest continues the very praise of Jesus.

The Bringing of the Wine

At the Last Supper, Jesus used red wine. Tradition kept this practice until the sixteenth century. At that time, a linen napkin called
the purificator was used to clean the chalice. White wine was pre-
ferred because it stains less than red wine.

Quite naturally, one watched over the quality of the wine des-
tined to become the blood of Christ. Gregory of Tours (†594) tells

---

[9] *General Instruction of the Roman Missal*, 283.

the story of a widow of Lyons who, throughout a year, had a Mass celebrated for her dead husband every day, *celebrans quotidie missarum solemnia*, bringing the necessary wine to the sacristy herself, *offerens oblationem pro memoria viri.* It was wine from Gaza, excellent wine, *vinum potentissimum.* Unfortunately, the subdeacon allowed himself to be tempted. He began to drink the good wine regularly and substituted a common, thin, acidic wine, *acetum* (vinegar). Since the pious widow did not receive communion every day, she did not notice the substitution until the day her husband appeared to her in a dream. He complained to his sweet wife *(Heu! Heu! Dulcissima coniux).* All his past work was not worth more to her than this detestable wine! The wife checked the next day. "Her teeth would have chattered if she had not swallowed it as quickly as possible."[10] The moral of the story is that it is necessary to receive communion at each Mass.

The Great Entrance
for the Mass of Easter Night

Let all mortal flesh keep silence,
and with fear and trembling stand.
Let no mortal thought enter into account.
For the King of kings, Christ our God, advances
to be sacrificed and given as food to the faithful.
Choirs of angels precede him,
with all the Principalities and Dominions,
the many-eyed Cherubim,
and the six-winged Seraphim.
They hide their faces and sing: Alleluia!

Liturgy of Saint James
Brightman, *Liturgies Eastern and Western,*
vol. 1, pp. 41–42.

---

[10] *Liber de gloria confessorum,* 65. PL 71,875 B—876 A.

The prayer for the wine, like the one for the bread, is inspired by the ancient Jewish blessing that Jesus pronounced over the cup:

> Blessed are you, Lord, God of all creation.
> Through your goodness we have this wine to offer,
> fruit of the vine and work of human hands.
> It will become our spiritual drink.

The Eastern liturgies have transformed the transfer of the gifts to the altar into a procession of solemn majesty. This procession is called the *Great Entrance* (*Megalē eisodos*) or the *Entrance of the Holy Mysteries* or the *Entrance of the Divine Gifts*. Preceded by torchbearers and surrounded by spirals of incense, the deacon and the priest leave the *prothèsis*, the table where the gifts or oblations are prepared, cross the nave and go to the altar. This procession of the oblations—which probably goes back to the seventh century—is thought to symbolize the entrance of Christ into Jerusalem, where he was going to suffer and rise again. The choir sings the lovely Cherubikon (hymn of the Cherubim):

> We who mystically represent the Cherubim
> and who sing the thrice-holy hymn
> to the life-giving Trinity,
> let us lay aside all earthly cares
> to welcome the King of the universe
> escorted invisibly by angelic hosts.[11]

In the Armenian liturgy,[12] the deacon and the priest express in dialogue fashion Ps 24:7-10:

> Lift up your heads, O you gates,
> be lifted up, you eternal doors!
> That the King of glory may enter!
>
> Who is the King of glory?
> He is the Lord of the universe!

The Roman liturgy has invented nothing equivalent. Here is a liturgical work to be opened, while still remaining in *sobrietas romana* (Roman sobriety).

---

[11] Brightman, *Liturgies Eastern and Western* (Oxford: Clarendon Press, vol.1, 1896), p. 122 (Liturgy of Saint Mark).

[12] *Ibid.*, pp. 431-432.

The Mixing of Water and Wine

The diluting of wine was a rather general practice in antiquity, both in the Greek and the Palestinian milieux. Sometimes it was even a necessity when the wine was heavy and thick. For the wine of Saron, which was particularly generous, one advised mixing one third wine to two thirds water.[13]

The gesture of adding a little water to the wine does not add anything to the beauty of the celebration. To give it meaning, it has been enriched with different symbolisms. The oldest symbolism which is found throughout the ages in different variations is proposed by Cyprian of Carthage (†258): "If someone offers only wine, the blood of Christ is without us. If someone offers only water, it is the people who are without Christ."[14]

The old prayer that the priest used to say while pouring the water was an echo of a prayer from the Christmas liturgy.[15] The new Order takes up this prayer while simplifying it: "By the mystery of this water and wine may we come to share in the divinity of Christ, who humbled himself to share in our humanity." The Ordo provides that the priest pour "a little water" and that he say the prayer inaudibly.

A rite fulfills its ministerial function only if it is performed clearly and if it is perfectly meaningful. Is that the case for this rite? Is a little drop of water poured quickly into some wine, which in our regions does not need any, apt to signify with grandeur and dignity the "admirable exchange" between Christ and humanity, an exchange which renders us participants in his divinity and in the eternity of his glory? This is a legitimate question.

Two Prayers, Witnesses of the Past

Two other prayers, through special privilege, have succeeded in remaining in the new Order of Mass. They are like agent witnesses of the old Offertory. By keeping them, the authorities were

---

[13] Strack-Billerbeck, *Kommentar zum Neuen Testament aus Talmud und Midrasch* (Munich: C. H. Beck) vol. IV, p. 58.

[14] *Epist. LXIII, Ad Caecilium,* CSEL, III, 711.

[15] J. A. Jungmann, *op. cit.* vol. 2, p. 339.

more sensitive to their emotions as a reminder of the past than to the immediate needs of the liturgy.

The first is a reminder of the ancient prayer *In spiritu humilitatis*. It recalls the prayers of apology: Bowing before the altar, the priest says inaudibly:

> Lord God, we ask you to receive us and be pleased with the sacrifice we offer you with humble and contrite hearts.

The second prayer is the one of the *Lavabo*. It is reduced to the minimum:

> Lord, wash away my iniquity;
> cleanse me from my sin.

The priest always says this prayer inaudibly and only for himself, for his own sins.

The rite of the *Lavabo* is difficult to celebrate and to interpret. If the priest needs to wash his hands because he received the gift of the faithful, he should do it seriously. A little drop of water on two fingers that are then wiped on a little handkerchief is hardly sufficient. On the other hand, he should not make this washing a celebratory act in front of the community. In our civilization, we do not wash our hands in public, much less at the family table, but rather somewhere in private.

Looking at the rites of the reformed Offertory, people have said: "Neither satisfaction without bounds . . . nor general reprobation."[16] Let us say that these last three prayers are supposed to be said *secreto*. Therefore, there is no cause to raise a flag in order to make them stand out. We can assume that they represent an intermediary stage toward another reform.

The Other Offerings: A Fraternal Sharing

Communion with Christ is lived in communion with all our brothers and sisters. The breaking of the bread of heaven includes the breaking of the bread of earth with all our brothers and sisters,

---

[16] N. K. Rasmussen, *Les rites de la présentation du pain et du vin*, in LMD 100 (1969), p. 58.

especially the poor and the needy. Paul recalls this with vehemence when he reproaches the Corinthians for claiming to share the "Lord's Supper" without accepting to share their own meal with the needy. What is this "Church of God" where one is hungry while another is drunk and where one humiliates those who have nothing? (1 Cor 11:20-22). Luke, on his part (Acts 5:34-35), describes the early community in idyllic terms: a community which finally realized the ideal of the messianic community described in Deut 15:4 in which no one was in need.

The Christian community is an heir of the Jewish tradition which practiced the service of charity each day by distributing "the bowl of the poor" for the needy passing through, and on the eve of the Sabbath by distributing "the bread of the poor"[17] for the needy of the land. It is normal that the Eucharistic celebration became the ideal place for this sharing of love. With the bread and the wine— from which one set apart what was necessary for the Eucharist— the faithful offered other gifts for the poor. The *Apostolic Tradition* (circa 215) mentions the offering of oil, cheese, olives, diverse fruits, and even flowers. All these gifts, offered either to the poor or to the bishop, were sanctified by the Eucharist. Tradition liked to see in the Eucharist the first fruits of creation.[18] From the eleventh century, money progressively replaced the gifts of nature. The collection is a legacy of this practice.

These offerings sometimes led to overestimating the meaning of the offertory. People offered to God all that could symbolize human joy and pain. There were touching excesses. On the feast of Saint Fiacre, the patron of market-gardeners, people brought bushels of vegetables into the sanctuary. On the feast of Saint Barbara they brought bunches of safety lamps. On the feast of veterans, they brought a forest of flags. Sometimes we find ourselves at the limits of folklore. At canonizations people offered the Pope two small casks of wine, candles, pigeons, and turtledoves in pretty cages.

These celebrations of the offertory are very fragile. It is not difficult to understand that God does not need vegetables, nor lamps,

[17] C. Perrot, *Jésus et l'Histoire* (Paris: Desclée, 1979), p. 296.
[18] Irenaeus of Lyons, *Against the Heresies*, IV, 17,5.

nor turtledoves. God tells us this with a sort of amused smile: "If I were hungry, I would not tell you, for the world is mine with all it contains. Do I eat the flesh of bulls or drink the blood of goats?" (Ps 50:12-13).

What God loves is that through these gifts the faithful render homage to God, that is, acknowledge that we are God's people, while giving God thanks: "Offer to God a sacrifice of thanksgiving" (Ps 50:14).

The Bread and the Wine

The use of bread and wine in the time of Jesus is inscribed in the context of the cultures of the Mediterranean Basin. This is true to such a point that in order to say "have a meal" one said "eat some bread" (Mark 3:20). One wonders if, in countries practicing different cultures, one could not use other elements to celebrate the Eucharist, for example cakes of manioc or millet and palm wine in Africa, or rice and tea in the Far East. Let us remember that two billion people use rice as their basic food and do not use wine as a drink. Let us simply think about the Moslem tradition which is opposed to wine. Are not the Moslems also called to share the Lord's Supper?

On the theological level, the problem is the following: Everything depends on the way one interprets the words of Jesus: "Do this in memory of me." If *this* means that it is necessary to take bread and wine, the Church obviously has no power to change the "matter" of the Eucharistic sacrifice. If *this* means that it is simply necessary to celebrate a meal, the Church can bring about the changes that she considers desirable.

What is the meaning of history in this domain? What evolution can we foresee, desire, hope for? The people of God, throughout their history, have always known how to assume the authentic human values that they met on their path toward the New Testament and to offer them to Christ. The incarnation of Jesus itself is the summit of this divinization of all human values.

Even today, inculturation, which is the incarnation of the Gospel into human values, and acculturation, which is the assumption of these values for the service of God, are missionary urgencies of primary importance.[19] The substitution for the bread and wine is only a very small problem with respect to the adaptation of the liturgy—and the entire Christian life—to the modern world.

Paul already said, with respect to the alimentary taboos of the Law, that he did not want to begin disputes over questions of vegetables when the Gospel was the real issue. Would Jesus want us to argue over questions of cereals and drinks when the entrance of the nations into the Kingdom is the real issue, when his love renders the Kingdom so close to us, so close precisely to the poorest, to those who, in the Third World, have only rice, manioc or millet for food? The answer that one gives to that question poses the problem—and furnishes the elements of response.

The Prayer Over the Gifts

A prayer over the gifts concludes the preparation of the gifts. The Gelasian Sacramentary[20] (circa 700) called it *Secreta*, "Secret," that is, prayer over the gifts that had been set apart (*secreta*, from *secernere*, "to separate," "to set apart") for the celebration of the Eucharist.

The meaning of this prayer is brought to light well by the following prayer:[21]

> Lord, our God,
> you wanted to choose in your creation
> bread and wine
> which renew our strength each day:
> make them also become for us
> the sacrament of eternal life.

The Door of Entry into the Eucharistic Offering

How can we sum up the meaning of the preparation of the bread and the wine?

[19] A. Chupungco, *Cultural Adaptation of the Liturgy* (New York/ Ramsey: Paulist Press, 1982). *La foi et l'inculturation*, Document of the International Theological Commission, DC 86 (1989), pp. 281–289.

[20] See M. Michaud, *Les livres liturgiques*, Coll. "Je sais-crois," 108 (1961), pp. 70–72.

[21] Cited by P. Jounel, *La Messe hier et aujourd'hui*, OEIL (1986), p. 106.

The Law requires: "No one will appear before me empty-handed
. . . You shall bring to the house of the Lord your God the best
of the firstfruits of your land (Exod 23:15, 19).

This Law was at the same time a prophecy. It announced the
Eucharist: we present ourselves to the Father, our hands full of this
perfect offering that is Christ Jesus, firstfruits of our earth.

The presentation of the gifts is the entrance into this offering
of the Eucharist.

2. THE EUCHARISTIC PRAYER

A. Introduction

Anaphora, Canon, Eucharistic Prayer

To designate the Eucharistic Prayer, the Eastern Liturgies prefer to use the word *Anaphora*. The Greek *anaphora* means "ascension" or "elevation," whence the more general meaning of offering
to God.

The Roman tradition used the word *Canon*. In Greek, *kanōn*
means "rule," from which we get the word "ruler," whence, by deri-
vation, "law," "principle," as in the expression "grammar rule." Thus
one said *canon actionis* to signify the law according to which the
liturgical action was to unfold. The expression evokes something
rigid, immutable. When Pope John XXIII introduced the name of
Saint Joseph into the Canon on November 13, 1962, the Christian
universe was astonished that he dared to touch the immutable
Canon.

The liturgical reform uses the expression *Eucharistic Prayer* (abbreviation: EP). That is the most suitable expression.

At the Sources of the Eucharistic Prayer

Just as the prayer of Jesus is rooted in the soil of Jewish prayer,
so does Christian prayer, and especially the Eucharistic Prayer,
which is the heart of its prayer, plunge its roots in the tradition
of Israel.

The First Description of the Mass
Circa 150

On the day named after the sun (that is, Sunday) all who live in city or countryside assemble.

The memoirs of the Apostles or the writings of the Prophets are read for as long as time allows.

When the lector has finished, the presider addresses us and exhorts us to imitate the splendid things we have heard.

Then we all stand and pray . . .

Then bread and a cup containing water and wine mixed with water are brought to the one who presides over the assembly.

He takes them, gives praise and glory to the Father of the universe, through the name of the Son and the Holy Spirit, and then makes a long "eucharist" (thanksgiving) for having been judged worthy of these good things.

When he is finished, all the people present give their assent with an "Amen!" ("Amen" in Hebrew means "So be it.")

When the presider has finished the Eucharist and all the people have signified their assent, those whom we call "deacons" distribute to each one present the consecrated bread, wine, and water; and they also carry them to those who are absent.

This food we call "Eucharist."

Apology, I, 65-66

The Jewish prayer which is the closest to the Eucharistic Prayer is the benediction *Yotser* which accompanied the daily recitation of the *Shema Israel*. It begins with the blessing of God the Creator, continues with a *Sanctus* and ends with prayers of intercession.[22]

---

[22] These prayers can be found in L. Deiss, *Springtime of the Liturgy*, p. 15 *(Yotser)*, pp. 73-77 *(Didache)*, pp. 123-127 (Hippolytus of Rome). For the original Greek or Latin text see Hänggi-Pahl, *Prex Eucharistica*, (Fribourg, Switzerland: Ed. Universitaires, 1968).

Eucharistic Prayer of the Didache

With regard to the Eucharist, give thanks in this way:
First, for the cup: "We give you thanks, our Father,
for the holy vine of David, your servant, which you have revealed
to us through Jesus, your Child.
   Glory to you for ever!"
Then for the bread broken: "We give you thanks, our Father,
for the life and knowledge which you have revealed to us
through Jesus, your Child.
   Glory to you for ever!"

Just as the bread broken,
was first scattered on the hills,
then was gathered and became one,
so let your Church be gathered
from the ends of the earth into your Kingdom!
For power and glory are yours for ever!"

Let no one eat or drink of your Eucharist
except those who have been baptized in the name of the Lord.
For it is of this that the Lord was speaking when he said:
"Do not give what is holy to dogs."

When your hunger has been satisfied, give thanks in this way:
"We thank you, holy Father,
for your holy name
which you have made to dwell in our hearts,
and for the knowledge, faith, and immortality
which you have revealed to us through Jesus, your Child.
   Glory to you for ever!"

All-powerful Master, you have created the universe
to the praise of your name;
you have given food and drink to the children of humanity
for their enjoyment;
but to us you graciously have bestowed a spiritual food
and drink for eternal life, through Jesus, your Child.

Above all, we thank you because you are almighty.

Glory to you for ever!
Amen.

Lord, remember your Church
and deliver it from all evil;
make it perfect in your love.

Gather together this sanctified Church from the four winds
into your kingdom which you have prepared for it.
For power and glory are yours for ever! Amen.

May the Lord come and this world pass away!
Amen.

Hosanna to the house of David!
If any are holy, let them come!
If any are not, let them repent.
Marana tha!
Amen.

Didache 9-10
Springtime of the Liturgy, pp. 74–76.

The Christian prayer which is the closest to the Eucharistic Prayer is the prayer of the *Didache*. The work that contains this prayer was discovered in 1875. Studies conducted for a century have not succeeded in penetrating its mystery. The least that can be said is that it is a matter of a prayer for a meal of *agape*, a meal which could have preceded the Eucharist (1 Cor 11:17-22). The most that can be affirmed is that it was indeed a Eucharistic Prayer of the Judeo-Christian community. One can grant the minimalist and maximalist position by concluding that the prayer belongs to an era when the Eucharist "was still celebrated and received in the context of a festive meal."[23] In spite of its great age—nearly twenty centuries of existence—this prayer keeps the fascinating beauty of its youth. Not a word has a wrinkle! Not a phrase has aged!

The oldest Eucharistic Prayer is the one of Hippolytus of Rome, in the *Apostolic Tradition* (circa 215). It presents a structure of solid

[23] G. Kretschmar, "La Liturgie ancienne dans les recherches actuelles," in *LMD* (1982), p. 81. See also *La Doctrine des Douze Apôtres*, SC 248 (1978), pp. 38–48.

First Eucharistic Prayer

Hippolytus of Rome (circa 215)

Acclamation Let the deacons present the oblation to the bishop. Laying hands upon it with all the presbytery, let him say the thanksgiving:

> The Lord be with you! Let all respond: And with your spirit! Let us lift up our hearts. They are turned to the Lord. Let us give thanks to the Lord! It is right and just!

Thanksgiving We give you thanks, O God, through your beloved Child, Jesus Christ, whom you sent to us in the last days as Savior, Redeemer, and Messenger of your will. He is your inseparable Word through whom you created everything and in whom you placed your kindness.

You sent him from heaven into the womb of a Virgin. He was conceived and became incarnate; he manifested himself as your Son, born of the Spirit and the Virgin.

He fulfilled your will, and, to acquire for you a holy people, he stretched out his hands in suffering to deliver from suffering those who believe in you.

Institution Narrative Before giving himself up to voluntary suffering in order to destroy death, to break the chains of the devil, to tread hell under his feet, to pour out his light upon the just, to establish the Covenant and manifest his Resurrection, he took bread; he gave you thanks and said: "Take, eat, this is my body which is broken for you." The same way for the cup, he said: "This is my blood which is poured out for you. When you do this, do (it) in memory of me."

Anamnesis Remembering, therefore, your death and your Resurrection, we offer you bread and wine, we give you thanks for having judged us worthy to stand before you and serve you.

Epiclesis   And we ask you to send your Holy Spirit on the offering of your holy Church, to bring together in unity all those who receive you. May they be filled with the Holy Spirit who strengthens their faith in the truth. May we be able thus to praise and glorify you through your Child, Jesus Christ.

Doxology   Through him, glory to you and honor to the Father and the Son, with the Holy Spirit, in your holy Church, now and for ever and ever! Amen.

Apostolic Tradition, 4.
L. Deiss, *Springtime of the Liturgy*, pp. 129–131.

and incomparable simplicity. At that time, the bishop still had the option of improvising the Eucharistic Prayer. Hippolytus writes with wisdom: "It is not necessary that the bishop take up the formulas which have been consigned higher up as though he had to force himself to say them by heart in his thanksgiving to God. Let each one pray according to his capacities. If someone is capable of praying a long time while uttering a solemn prayer, that is good . . . provided that his prayer is sound and conforms to orthodoxy."[24]

In the fourth and fifth centuries, the oral tradition of the Eucharistic Prayer was fixed in written formulas. The Eucharistic Prayers of this period of great literary creativity spring up in the field of the liturgy like daffodils in spring. For the East, let us point out the one of Serapion (†circa 362), bishop of Thmuis in Lower Egypt, and the one of the *Apostolic Constitutions* (circa 380) of unbelievable length. The masterpiece of these Eucharistic Prayers is incontestably the Anaphora of Saint Basil. In the West, the Latin tradition produced the Canon of which Saint Ambrose (†397) attests the first elements.

The Four Eucharistic Prayers

The reform gave birth to numerous creations of Eucharistic Prayer. Some are "wild" creations. Others have been approved by

[24] *Apostolic Tradition*, 9.

Rome for special circumstances.[25] Four have been retained for the Missal for ordinary Masses.

EUCHARISTIC PRAYER I

Eucharistic Prayer I is based on the old Roman Canon. It dates from the fourth century, at the time when Greek was definitively abandoned in Rome for Latin. Its oldest vestiges are read in the treatise *De Sacramentis*[26] that Saint Ambrose drafted around 378. It appears fixed in a definitive way around the seventh century. From the eleventh and twelfth centuries, it became the only Canon of the entire Church of the West. It reigned in an absolute manner until November 30, 1969 (the date the new Missal came into use), therefore for about fifteen centuries. For almost fourteen centuries, it was even forbidden to translate it. It was recited silently, and the Council of Trent[27] anathematized whoever dared to criticize this silent recitation *(submissa voce)* of the presidential prayer or to affirm that it should be said in the "vulgar" language. These are old memories.

People have often praised its literary beauty, the simplicity of its nobility, the inviolability of its antiquity, "the aura of mystery" that emanates from it, "the holy fear" that it inspires.[28] It was considered as a sanctuary—people sometimes said the Holy of Holies—into which the priest alone could enter. The old Ordo I writes: *Surgit pontifex solus et intrat in canone*, the bishop arises alone and enters into the Canon.[29]

No doubt the veneration with which the old formulas are surrounded worked when the reform did not want or did not dare to renovate the Canon in depth. In spite of the beauty of certain prayers—especially the two that follow the consecration—in spite of the finesse of the translation which knew how to lighten the text, it appears to us today a little heavy and incoherent. The mass of

[25] See *Eucharisties de tous pays* (Paris: Centre National de Pastorale liturgique, 1973).

[26] *Sources Chrétiennes*, 25 bis (1961), Editions du Cerf, pp. 114–118.

[27] Denzinger-Schönmetzer, #1759.

[28] C. Vagaggini, in *LMD*, 87 (1966), p. 134. By the same author: *Le Canon de la Messe*, Coll. "Lex Orandi," 41 (1967).

[29] J. A. Jungmann, *op. cit.*, vol. 3, p. 8.

prayers, the repeated alternation of thanksgiving and invocations give the impression of an "agglomeration with no apparent unity,"[30] of a text that does not progress because it does not know where it wants to go.

Sometimes we venerate the sacredness of the ancient formulas to such a point that we no longer use them. We can ask ourselves if this is not the danger that threatens the old Roman Canon.

EUCHARISTIC PRAYER II

This Eucharistic Prayer is an adaptation of the oldest Eucharistic Prayer, the one of Hippolytus of Rome. It has been enriched with the *Sanctus* (that it did not possess) as well as with an invocation to the Holy Spirit before the consecration. After almost fifteen centuries of oblivion, this old prayer reappeared in the Roman liturgy, adorned with incomparable youth. This is the shortest Eucharistic Prayer: no useless word, no redundancy in the sentences. It is a model of clarity and logic.

Note the extreme humility of the sentence:

> We thank you for counting us worthy
> to stand in your presence and serve you.

EUCHARISTIC PRAYER III

Eucharistic Prayer III is a recasting of a draft of a Eucharistic Prayer that had been worked out by the Consilium on the Liturgy as an alternate prayer of the Canon.[31] Since it is a new composition, it reveals clearly the structure that was considered ideal for the Eucharistic Prayer. Here it is:

> Dialogue of Introduction and Preface
>   Sanctus and Post-Sanctus
>   Epiclesis
>   Account of the Institution and anamnesis
>   Epiclesis
>   Intercessions
> Final doxology

---

[30] C. Vagaggini, *Le Canon de la Messe*, Coll. "Lex Orandi," 41 (1967), p. 86.
[31] See C. Vagaggini, *Le Canon de la Messe*, pp. 121–154.

This Eucharistic Prayer is without doubt the most elaborate on the theological level. It underlines the action of the Holy Spirit (in the Post-Sanctus and the two epicleses); it vigorously attests to the sacrificial aspect of the Eucharist (perhaps to face in advance the criticisms of the traditionalists); it also affirms with beauty our participation in the offering of Christ:

"May he make us an everlasting gift to you."

EUCHARISTIC PRAYER IV

Eucharistic Prayer IV draws its inspiration from Eastern anaphoras, especially from the one of Saint Basil (330?-379).

Its particular beauty resides in its first part, from the Preface to the first epiclesis. It celebrates the eternity of God the Creator, it sings his holiness with the angels, it acclaims the plan of God which goes from the creation of Adam to the birth of Jesus, to his death, and to his resurrection. It is a jubilant melody, without fault, which links the eternity of God to the salvation of humanity in a unique song of love.

B. THE FULL EXTENT OF THE EUCHARISTIC PRAYER

Dialogue of Introduction

All the Eucharistic Prayers begin with a dialogue of introduction. It is possible that this custom is a legacy of the Jewish tradition. The oldest witness of this dialogue is read in the Eucharistic Prayer of Hippolytus.

According to the old canon, the priest enters alone into the Canon, but he is accompanied spiritually by the entire community. He is going to say the Eucharistic Prayer alone, but the entire community prays it with him in spirit. The dialogue of introduction attests to the unity of the celebrating community.

Saint Cyprian, in his treatise on prayer, which dates from the years 251-252, adds this other reason: "When we rise for the prayer, beloved brothers, we must watch and apply ourselves with all our hearts to prayer. Let all carnal and worldly thoughts be cast aside, let the soul think of nothing other than praying." And it is really for that reason that the priest, before the Eucharistic Prayer, prepares the spirit of the brothers by saying in the Preface: "Let us lift up our hearts!" The people respond: "We turn them to the Lord." We are exhorted in this way to think of nothing other than the Lord.[32]

Thanksgiving or Preface

The real presence of Christ in the Eucharist, with the account of the Institution, had formerly absorbed all the attention of Christian piety. The Preface was considered as a sort of introduction, an appetizer without much importance, as some prefaces in books sometimes are.

In reality, the Preface *(praefatio)* is not a *discourse (fatio)* that one says *before (prae)* the Canon, but really the thanksgiving that one proclaims *before* the community. "It is a poem, the cry of joy and recognition, the song of the world discovering its salvation, . . . the certitude of faith making hope spring forth, as had to have been the prayer of Jesus on the night of Holy Thursday."[33] The Prefaces of the Anaphora of Hippolytus and that of Addai and Mari are excellent witnesses of this praise born in the environment of the Jewish benediction.

How difficult it is to say thank you to God in a Preface which pleases all communities, at all times, all sensibilities, and which is at the same time "a poem, the cry of joy and recognition, the song of the world!" It can be asked: Is this even possible? In any case, we must not be surprised if some Prefaces of the Missal, especially those which are born in modern time, lay themselves open to criticism, get lost in the intellectual abstraction of a theology course, and give rise only to a bored silence. Others, it has been said, founder "in the marsh of sentimental piety" or become intoxicated with the "clanking of their learned formulas."[34] Even the most venerated formulas of antiquity can seem cold and dull to us. How can we expect our good people, who know the taste of bread and wine, who admire the beauty of a flower, the splendor of a mountain the infinity of the sea, who know how to thank God for the love of a

---

[32] *De Dominica Oratione*, 31.
[33] Ph. Béguerie, *Eucharisties de tous pays*, CNPL, 1973, p. 8.
[34] L. Bouyer, "La Préface et le Sanctus" in *LMD*, 87 (1966), p. 103.

wife and the joy of children, how can we expect these people, I say, to become enthused when we say to them that God the Father, through the glory of Jesus, "has renewed humanity in his immortal image" (Preface of Epiphany)! Other formulas of "modern" making, which circulate in certain communities, even if they harpoon our attention and stir our heart, leave us hungry nevertheless. Of course, we can give thanks to God for having given us Jesus, "that unforgettable man"[35]; but is that the entirety of the mystery of Jesus? Yes, how difficult it is then to say thanks to God in a praise that is suitable to all sensibilities!

Formerly, each Mass could have its Preface (the Leonine Sacramentary counts 269 of them). Today, the reform has set out again on the path of true tradition. Thus the book of Masses in honor of the Virgin Mary[36] proposes a new Preface for each one of the 46 masses presented in it. Therefore the reform is on the right track. The site of the creation of new Prefaces should remain open. For much creativity and patience are needed to give birth to a single masterpiece.

Sanctus,
Acclamation of the Universe

THE BIBLICAL TEXT

The Sanctus is presented as a cento of biblical texts.[37]

> Holy, holy, holy Lord,
> God of power and might (Isa 6:3; Rev 4:8),
> heaven and earth are full of your glory (Isa 6:3).
> Hosanna in the highest (Matt 21:9; Mark 11:10).

> Blessed is he who comes
> *in the name of the Lord* (Ps 118:26; Matt 21:9; Mark 11; Luke 19:38).
> *Hosanna in the highest* (Matt 21:9; Mark 11:10).

---

[35] H. Osterhuis, *Quelqu'un parmi nous* (Paris: Desclée, 1966), p. 118.

[36] *Collection of Masses of the Blessed Virgin Mary* (Collegeville, Minn.: The Liturgical Press, 1992). In Masses for special groups, one can enrich the official text through special thanksgiving expressing the celebrating community.

[37] Analysis in *Spirit and Song of the New Liturgy*, pp. 82–87.

The first two acclamations are borrowed from the account of the vision which will inaugurate the ministry of Isaiah around the year 740 B.C. The prophet is in the Temple. The heavens open before him and God appears to him in glory. The Seraphim, beings of fire and light, serve as acolytes at the divine throne. Carried away by ecstasy, Isaiah hears their song:

> Holy, holy, holy is the Lord Almighty!
> The earth is full of his glory (Isa 6:3).

To the Seraphim of Isaiah, the liturgy likes to associate myriads of angels. The anaphora of Serapion, bishop of Thmuis, in Lower Egypt around 350, does this with generosity:

> You are attended by thousands upon thousands and myriads upon myriads of Angels and Archangels, of Thrones and Dominions, of Principalities and Powers. Beside you stand the two august Seraphim . . . They sing your holiness. With theirs, receive also our acclamation to your holiness.[38]

The text of Isaiah reads: "*The earth* is full of his glory." The liturgy substitutes: "*Heaven and earth* are full of your glory." The perspective is enlarged; it is immense. It is both on earth and in heaven that the angels and humanity, along with all of creation, unite in a common exultation for the eternal celebration of the Father. The liturgy appears clearly like the descent of the Eternal into time, or like the insertion of earthly acclamation into the praise of heaven. To the question: Is the cosmic universe, with its millions of stars and its millions of light-years, interested in our Eucharist, the liturgy answers: Yes, for Christ is the firstborn of creation. To the question: Are the myriads of angels present in our acclamation to the divine glory, the liturgy answers: Yes, because all spiritual creatures were created "in him, . . . through him, and for him" (Col 1:16).

Hosanna comes from the Hebrew and literally means: "Give salvation." The word comes from Ps 118:25: "Give salvation, Lord, give!" It was used consequently as an acclamation of praise. On the Feast of Tents, people made a procession with palms while sing-

---

[38] Deiss, *Springtime of the Liturgy*, p. 194.

ing "Hosanna." The seventh day was called the Great Hosanna.

In the highest is a Hebrew expression. It means: Hosanna to God who lives in the highest of heavens.

Blessed is he who comes is likewise borrowed from Ps 118:26. It is a matter of a blessing uttered over a pilgrim who was entering the Temple. Tradition transformed the acclamation " Blessed be, in the name of the Lord, the one who comes" into a messianic acclamation: "Blessed be the One-who-comes in the name of the Lord." In the New Testament, the One-who-comes, *ho erchomenos*, is a messianic title of Christ.

When Jesus made his solemn entrance into Jerusalem, the crowd of disciples, holding the palms that they had gathered in Ps 118:27, acclaim him:

> Hosanna to the Son of David!
> Blessed be He who comes in the name of the Lord!
> Hosanna in the highest (of heavens)! (Matt 21:9)

The biblical climate of our Sanctus is one of a celebration of glory. A royal theophany of the God of Hosts, myriads of angels who surround the Lord, cosmic praise to the Master of the universe, heavenly glory invading the earth, royal liturgy of the Feast of Tents, jubilation of the day of Palms, parousia of the Messiah who comes in the name of the Lord: it is all this ambiance of a feast that the Sanctus should evoke. The Sanctus whispered softly by parsimonious voices, stingily saving their breath, singing an adagio on the "Blessed is he who comes in the name of the Lord," is, if one can say so, outside of the text. The singing of Isaiah's Seraphim made the hinges of the threshold of the Temple vibrate!

THE SANCTUS IN THE EUCHARISTIC PRAYER

You recall that the Eucharistic Prayer of Hippolytus did not have the Sanctus. How then did it enter into the Eucharistic Prayer? No doubt this happened through a sort of osmosis or imitation of a Jewish prayer. The *Yotser*,[39] a benediction that accompanies the

---

[39] *Ibid.*, pp. 15–16.

recitation of the *Shema Israel*, is actually made up of blessings, of a *Sanctus*, and of prayers of intercession. That is the oldest structure of our Eucharistic Prayer:

(Blessing)
You are blessed, Lord our God, King of the universe,
you who form the light and create the darkness, who
shed the light of your mercy upon the earth and those who dwell
on it, who, out of goodness,
unceasingly renew every day the works of your creation . . .

(Sanctus)
May your name be glorified for eternity, our king, who create the
angels . . . They bless, they magnify,
they adore, they proclaim:
    Holy, holy, holy is the Lord Sabaoth!
    The earth is full of his glory . . .
    Blessed be the glory of the Lord!

(Intercession)
Illumine Zion with a new light!
Let us soon be worthy of your light!

If the dignity of a song is measured with respect to its relationship and its proximity with the Eucharist, the Sanctus, which is situated at the heart of the liturgical action, is the most important acclamation of the Eucharistic Prayer. Or further: if the community sang only one song, this should be the Sanctus.

The Sanctus is the song of unity: ". . . we join the angels and the saints in proclaiming your glory" (Eucharistic Prayer II) "and in the name of every creature under heaven" (Eucharistic Prayer IV). The General Instruction affirms:

Joining with the angels, the congregation sings or recites the *Sanctus*. This acclamation is an intrinsic part of the eucharistic prayer and all the people join with the priest in singing or reciting it.[40]

A symphony of unity, the Sanctus gathers together into one praise the cosmic universe, the angelic world, the saints of heaven, and the Church of the earth.

---

[40] *General Instruction of the Roman Missal*, 55b.

TOWARD THE LITURGY OF HEAVEN

According to Revelation, the Sanctus is the acclamation of the heavenly liturgy. It is said: "Day and night the angels do not cease repeating: Holy, holy, holy, the Lord, God of the universe, The One-who-was, Who-is, and Who-comes."

Each Eucharist on earth invites us to travel towards this eternal praise of the liturgy of heaven.

Post-Sanctus:
"You Are Holy Indeed"

In the second, third, and fourth Eucharistic Prayers, this prayer links the Sanctus to the epiclesis. The second Eucharistic prayer states: "Lord, you are holy indeed, the fountain of all holiness." This is a perfect example of a filler text which serves as a link.

In the fourth Eucharistic Prayer, this prayer continues the thanksgiving of the Preface.

Fortunately, the French Missal has enriched the "filler text" for the second and third Eucharistic Prayer with formulas suitable for Sundays, weekly feasts of the Resurrection, for the time of the Nativity, and for Easter week. Here is a prayer provided for Easter week (the text added to the early text is in italics).

> You are holy indeed, the fountain of all holiness,
> *here we are gathered before you,*
> *and, in communion with the entire Church,*
> *we celebrate the very holy day when our Lord Jesus Christ*
> *rose according to the flesh.*
> *Through him, whom you have raised to your right,*
> *God our Father, we pray to you.*

Epiclesis of Consecration:
"Pour Out Your Holy Spirit. . ."

Epiclesis literally means *invocation klēsis upon (épi).* In liturgical vocabulary, the epiclesis is the invocation of the Holy Spirit either *upon the offerings* "so that they may become for us the body and blood of our Lord, Jesus Christ" (Eucharistic Prayer II) or *upon the community* itself so that it may share in the fruits of the Eucharist, so that it may be "brought together in unity by the Holy Spirit" (Eucharistic Prayer II). The first epiclesis is called epiclesis of consecration; the second, epiclesis of communion.

The Eastern anaphoras often bind these two epicleses into a single prayer. Here is the epiclesis of the Anaphora of Saint Basil:

> May your Holy Spirit come upon us, your servants,
> and upon these gifts that you have given to us,
> may he sanctify them and make them the holy
> food destined for the saints.

> May this bread become the body of our Lord, God,
> and Savior Jesus Christ, for remission of sins
> and eternal life for those who receive it.
> May this cup become the precious blood of the New Covenant
> of our Lord, God, and Savior Jesus Christ,
> for the remission of sins and eternal life
> for those who receive it.

The first Eucharistic Prayer, which takes up the old Canon, does not present an explicit invocation to the Holy Spirit. One considers the prayer *Bless and approve our offering* which immediately precedes the account of the Institution as having epicletic value.

Eucharistic Prayers II, III, and IV, following the anaphora of Saint Mark,[41] place the epiclesis right before the account of the Institution. Eucharistic Prayer III which, as you recall, is a recent creation, shows well the meaning that the Church gives to the epiclesis:

> And so, Father, we bring you these gifts.
> We ask you to make them holy by the power of your Spirit,
> that they may become the body + and blood
> of your Son, our Lord, Jesus Christ.

As for the epiclesis of communion, Eucharistic Prayers II, III, and IV place it after the anamnesis which follows the consecration.

---

[41] The Anaphora of St. Mark presents evidence of the anaphoras used in the Church of Egypt. Some elements of this anaphora go back to the fourth-fifth century. The Greek text with a Latin translation can be found in Hänggi-Pahl, *Prex Eucharistica*, pp. 102–115.

THE MOMENT OF CONSECRATION

According to Eastern tradition, it is the epiclesis which consecrates the bread and wine into the body and blood of the risen Christ. According to Western tradition, it is the narration of the Institution that performs this consecration. Popular belief has sometimes even exaggerated the quasi-magical and instantaneous power of the words called consecratory. It used to be affirmed that when the priest said: *Hoc* (this): there was nothing. *Est* (is): there was nothing. *Enim* (indeed): there was nothing. *Corpus* (the body): still nothing. *Meum* (of mine): there was everything, there was the body of Christ. A story is told about a priest who left the Church in modern times. He entered a bakery, pronounced the sacred words, and consecrated the entire bakery (a belief contrary to all sane theology, since in order to perform a sacrament, the priest must want to do what the Church wants to be done, which was obviously not the case). In popular language we even say: "Do hocus pocus" (abbreviation of "Hoc est corpus"), to signify: do a conjuring trick.

Actually, the question of the precise moment of the consecration, quite like the discussion of the consecratory value of the epiclesis or of the narration of the Institution, is a bad question. It arose at the turn of the thirteenth-fourteenth century in the course of the controversies between the East and the West.[42] And a badly posed problem cannot receive a correct solution. In reality, the Eucharistic Prayer forms a unity of praise, blessing, thanksgiving, and request. It is the entirety of this prayer which is consecratory. That is so true that the old Roman Canon (actually Eucharistic Prayer I), which does not have an explicit epiclesis, is perfectly valid, as is the Anaphora of Addai and Mari, which does not have a narration of Institution (see pp. 82–83).

WHO CONSECRATES?

The epiclesis underlines with superb precision the humility of the priestly ministry. Sometimes it is said that the priest consecrates.

---

[42] See Nicholas Cabasilas (fourteenth century), in SC 4 bis (1967), pp. 31–36. Concerning this whole question see Y. Congar, *Je crois en l'Esprit Saint*, vol. III (Paris: Cerf, 1980), pp. 294–330.

Strictly speaking, the affirmation does not hold up. In any case, the epiclesis reveals exactly what the priest does: he says the prayer through which the celebrating community asks the Father to send his Holy Spirit over the bread and wine so that they may become the body and blood of Jesus. Eucharistic Prayer III says explicitly:

> And so, Father, we bring you these gifts.
> We ask you to make them holy
> by the power of your Spirit,
> that they may become the body and blood
> of your Son, our Lord Jesus Christ.

Therefore it is the Father who consecrates through his Spirit. The priest merely says the prayer, in the name of the community.

The epiclesis is also a hymn of praise to the Trinity. The Father is at the center of this praise. He sent his Holy Spirit over the Virgin Mary so that the body of Jesus might spring forth in her: he sends his Spirit again over the offering of the community so that it may become the body of the risen Christ. The community welcomes this grace and gives glory to the Father, through the Son, in the Spirit.

Account of the Institution:
"The Lord Jesus, on the Night He Was Betrayed. . ."

At the heart of the Eucharistic Prayer is situated the account of the Institution.

THE BIBLICAL TEXT

The account of the Institution comes to us according to four different recensions: the one of Paul in 1 Cor 11:23-25, the one of Matt 26:26-28, the one of Mark 14:22-24, and the one of Luke 22:19-20.

The synopsis of the texts allows us to distinguish clearly the group of Paul and Luke and the group of Matthew and Mark. We are inclined to think that the recension of Paul and Luke, whose Greek is better, represents the tradition of the Church of Antioch, and the group of Mark (whose text divulges more the Semitic original) and of Matthew represents the tradition of the Palestinian

Church. Each tradition can contain elements very close to the original.

Paul's stay in Corinth goes back to the years 50–52. Paul himself refers to an anterior tradition which was given to him: "For I have received what I in turn passed on to you" (1 Cor 11:23). The testimony that he cites can therefore go back to the first years of Christianity (perhaps to the year 40).

THE LITURGICAL TEXT

The liturgy, always in search of beauty, has embellished the evangelical text. Indeed, no Eucharistic Prayer adhered literally to the text of Scripture. The sublime simplicity of the evangelical account, whose grandeur comes uniquely from the very act of Jesus, not from the words that tell about it, is somewhat veiled by literary redundancy. Instead of saying: "Jesus took bread and gave it to them," one affirms: "He took bread in his holy, pure, blessed, and life-giving hands and gave it to his beloved apostles" (Coptic Liturgy). No doubt Eastern sensibility finds itself at ease in such grandiloquence.

The first Eucharistic Prayer did not want to touch up the text of the old Canon. It kept its solemn heaviness. It says that Jesus took *"hunc praeclarum calicem in sanctas ac venerabiles manus suas."* That means, "Jesus took this eminent cup in his holy and venerable hands." It can be asked if it was opportune to keep such grandiloquence, a reflection of the taste of another epoch and far removed from the simplicity of the Gospel. When the priest looks at his own hands, he knows that they are neither holy nor venerable, but sinful; and when he celebrates in missionary countries with a cup made out of wood or baked earth, he can only smile while affirming that this cup is eminent.

The second, third, and fourth Eucharistic Prayers have kept the humble beauty of the evangelical text. The second Eucharistic Prayer is certainly the most successful:

> [Jesus] took bread and gave you thanks.
> He broke the bread,
> gave it to his disciples and said:

"Take this, all of you, and eat it:
this is my body which will be given up for you."

The fourth Eucharistic Prayer adds that Jesus "blessed" the bread and the cup. It must be understood that Jesus blessed God while pronouncing the blessing over the bread and the wine according to the formulas of the Jewish tradition.

Among the new Eucharistic Prayers, the one proposed for the native population of Australia finds again, with simple words, the transparency of the Gospel:

A long time ago,
the night before he was going to die,
Jesus and his friends had a meal together.
He blessed you, Father,
he broke the bread and said to his friends:
"Take this, all of you: this is my body.
Tomorrow I will die for you."[43]

THE PARTICIPATION OF THE ASSEMBLY

In the Roman liturgy, the assembly does not intervene directly into the narration of the Institution. The monologue of the priest underlines the specific nature of the sacerdotal ministry: only the priest says the consecratory prayer.

In the Eastern liturgies, the assembly supports the prayer of the priest with its acclamations. The Coptic liturgy creates a true festive climate at the heart of the narration of the Institution:

Having resolved to give himself up to death
for the life of the world,
We believe that this is the truth. Amen!
He took bread into his holy, pure, blessed,
and life-giving hands,
We believe that this is the truth. Amen!
He lifted up his eyes to heaven to you, his Father
and the Lord of the universe. He gave thanks,
Amen!
He blessed it,

---

[43] *Eucharisties de tous pays*, p. 43.

Amen!
He sanctified it,
Amen, amen, amen! We believe, we confess, we glorify.
He broke it and gave it to his beloved apostles saying to them:
This is my body which will be broke
for many for remission of sins. Do this in memory of me.
We believe that this is the truth. Amen![44]

The same acclamations are found for the consecration of the wine. In the Middle Ages, it was affirmed boldly: "The priest does not sacrifice alone, does not consecrate alone, but the entire assembly of faithful who attend consecrates with him, sacrifices with him."[45] Father Congar confirms: "The entire liturgical assembly is celebrating and consecrating." And he adds: "But it would be an ecclesiological error and a liturgical heresy to have the words of consecration said by the entire assembly. It has its "president," who functions as president. And yet it is entirely sacerdotal and celebrating."[46]

It remains for our Roman liturgy to find paths for expressing the mystery of the assembly which consecrates through the ministry of its priest. For if the account of the Institution is the heart of the Eucharistic Prayer, it is really there, at the heart of this prayer, that the community must express its presence.

The Mystery of the Word and the Community

The account of the Institution is the most sublime example of the actualization of the Word of God. In fact, it is a matter of a reading of a biblical text, a reading similar to the one of the Gospel. But this reading realizes at the same time what it signifies: the Word becomes action, it changes the bread and the wine into Eucharist. No other part in the celebration verifies better what Jesus proclaimed in the synagogue of Nazareth: "Today is fulfilled for you the word that you have just heard" (Luke 4:21)

---

[44] *Notre Messe copte* (Cairo: Ed. du Foyer Catholique, 1967), pp. 62–65.
[45] Attributed to Guerric D'Igny, *Sermo 5,15;* PL 185,87 B; cited by Y. Congar, Vatican II, Coll. "Unam Sanctam," 66 (1967), p. 252. Concerning authenticity, see T. Morson and H. Costello, *Dictionnaire de la Spiritualité,* vol. 6, col. 1115, p. 252.
[46] Y. Congar, *Le Concile de Vatican II,* Collection "Théologie Historique," 71 (1984), Ed. du Cerf, p. 113.

This Word-action is also a Word-prayer. In reality the narration is proclaimed before the community, but it is at the same time addressed to God. Reading the evangelical text, the priest says that Jesus lifted up his eyes "to you, his almighty Father, he gave you thanks and praise" (Eucharistic Prayer I). The Word-action is therefore a memorial of the prayer of Jesus.

The Word manifests here the plenitude of its power. And yet, the celebratory act of the community (it is celebrating the Lord's Supper) is more important than the Word of the Institution (it says

---

Anaphora of Addai and Mari
(Beginning of the third century)

We give you thanks, Lord, for the abundant riches of your grace toward us. For when we were sinners and weak, you made us worthy, according to your great mercy, to celebrate the holy mysteries of the body and blood of your Christ.

We implore the help that comes from you. Strengthen our souls so that we may celebrate with perfect charity and sincere love the gift that you have given us.

We praise you, we glorify you, we give you thanks, we adore you now and always and for ever and ever . . .

It is right that all mouths give glory, that all tongues give thanks to the adorable and glorious name of the Father, of the Son, and of the Holy Spirit. He created the world according to his grace and those who dwell in it, according to his mercy. He saved humanity according to his mercy; he filled mortal flesh with his great grace.

Your majesty, Lord, a thousand heavenly spirits adore, as well as myriads of myriads of angels, the ranks of spirits, the servants of fire and spirit. With the Cherubim and the other Seraphim they glorify your name, they cry out and give glory.

Syriac anaphora (Eastern Syria)
L. Deiss, *Springtime of the Liturgy*, p. 15

that it is celebrating it): that is the teaching of the Syriac anaphora of the Apostles Addai and Mari.[47]

This very ancient anaphora (perhaps from the beginning of the third century), very close to Jewish blessings, has a prodigious history. It is unique, unclassifiable in the sense that it does not have an account of the Institution. Before this "anomaly," which unnerved the sagacity of the historians of the liturgy and troubled the good working of theories, the hypothesis was put forth—that was the easiest thing to do—that the account of the Institution figured well in the primitive text but had been lost later through the corruption of the text or ulterior arrangements.

While the liturgical world dozed on a pillow of idleness, dreaming that the affair was definitely shelved, W. F. Macomber, digging in the libraries of the Middle East, had the extraordinary luck to discover manuscripts five centuries older than those which we had in our possession, which gave the anaphora in its oldest form. He published it in 1966. Amazingly, it was confirmed that the Anaphora of Addai and Mari had never had an account of the Institution. Therefore, one could celebrate the Lord's Supper without saying the narration that tells about it.

We are invited to admit that in the third-fourth centuries, a double tradition existed in the regions placed in the liturgical movement of Syria: one tradition that attached great importance to the account of the Institution and another tradition, of East Syria, that attached the same importance to the epiclesis and did not use the account of the Institution.[48] The teaching is the following: the fact that the community is authentically celebrating the Lord's Supper can be signified not only through words (those of the Institution that are recited), but through the liturgical action itself. In the case of the Anaphora of Addai and Mari, the "do" is more important than the "say."

This teaching is always valid. A community is "eucharistic" not so much because it says that it celebrates the Eucharist, but by the fact that it lives it.

---

[47] Deiss, *Springtime of the Liturgy*, pp. 157–163.
[48] E. Lanne, *Dictionnaire de Spiritualité*, vol. IX, col. 900.

THE ELEVATION

At the beginning of the thirteenth century began the practice of elevating the host after the consecration, and at the end of the thirteenth century, the priest elevated the chalice. Popular belief attached great importance to this elevation at precisely a time when people received Eucharistic communion less and less. It was thought that whoever looked at the host during the elevation was preserved on that day from sudden death, and his house and barn were sheltered from fire. Also, when the priest did not raise the host high enough, the most fervent groaned or called out: "Higher! Higher!"

Today the elevation offers the Christian people the opportunity to express their faith in Christ by worshipping him silently: "My Lord and my God!"

Anamnesis:
"We Remember Your Death and Your Resurrection"

Anamnesis is from the Greek *anamnēsis*, which means "remembrance, commemoration." At the Last Supper Christ had asked: "Do this in memory of me—*eis tēn emēn anamnēsin*" (Luke 22:19). The prayer of the anamnesis responds to the request of Christ. It unfolds in four sections.

First, there is the formula of introduction said by the priest. "Let us proclaim the mystery of faith."

Then, there is the anamnesis of the assembly: it commemorates the death and resurrection of Jesus and proclaims his return in glory.

There is the anamnesis of the priest.

Finally, there is a prayer of offering and thanksgiving of the priest. The prayer of Eucharistic Prayer II is formulated in this way:

> We offer you, Father,
> this life-giving bread, this saving cup.
> We thank you for counting us worthy
> to stand in your presence
> and serve you.

STRUCTURE

The structure of this acclamation, so happily restored to the assembly, somewhat lacks precision.

In fact, the first element, the invitation to the acclamation ("Let us proclaim the mystery of faith") seems useless. One does not introduce an acclamation: one acclaims spontaneously. Has anyone seen people ask for an acclamation for a touchdown at a football game? The eucharistic acclamation should spring forth from the assembly even more spontaneously, since it is the community itself which is celebrating its victory in the resurrection of Christ. Actually, the expression "mystery of faith" was found in the old Canon. It was taken away from the account of the Institution. It was inserted here. Its insertion weighs down the prayer.

The third element, the anamnesis of the priest, is also somewhat surprising. Would the priest not have heard what the assembly said or would he consider himself outside of the assembly so that he in turn makes his own anamnesis? His prayer, a doublet of the one of the assembly, does not make the celebration move on, but slows it down.

It can reasonably be supposed that the new Eucharistic Prayers originally presented only the anamnesis of the priest. As in the old Canon, one passed quite naturally from the account of the Institution to the anamnesis: "That is why, remembering . . ." Later, in order to promote the participation of the assembly, which is an excellent thing, the anamnesis of the assembly was introduced, but without harmonizing it with the priest. Just as we easily discover the improvements that were brought to the original plans of a house in order to make the dwelling more habitable, thus we likewise note the improvements that the reform introduced into the liturgical texts to make the prayer more beautiful. One could further say that these improvements are like scars of esthetic surgery that the reform performed on the texts. They are the price of beauty.

THE SONG OF THE HOLY SPIRIT

The anamnesis is the prayer of the Holy Spirit in us. Jesus had said: "The Holy Spirit that the Father will send in my name will teach you everything and will remind you (*hypomnēsei*) of everything that I said to you" (John 14:26). The Spirit is the memory of the Church. He reminds us unceasingly of the Passover of the Lord, that is, the mystery of his death and his resurrection.

The Spirit also opens for us the door upon the future of the Church: "He will tell you what must come" (John 16:13), that is, the glorious return of Jesus at the end of time.

The anamnesis is the song of the Holy Spirit at the heart of the assembly.

Epiclesis of Communion: "Send Your Holy Spirit Upon Us"

As was said previously (p. 76), the epiclesis of communion is the invocation of the Holy Spirit upon the celebrating community so that it may share in the fruits of the Eucharist. Two graces are especially requested: that the community may be gathered together in a single body and that it may become an eternal offering to the glory of the Father.

Every grace originates as in its source in the love of the "Father of lights" (Jas 1:17). It is earned for us by Christ. It is given to us by the Holy Spirit: he is, par excellence, *Donum Dei*, the Gift of God to messianic times.

Intercessions: "Remember, Lord"

One can be astonished at the presence of new prayers of intercession after the epiclesis of communion: have we not interceded enough at the time of the Prayer of the Faithful? Actually, the Eucharistic Prayer follows the bipartite structure of the old Jewish blessing: thanksgiving and request. It could be affirmed that the Eucharistic Prayer is nothing but the Jewish prayer at the center of which one has intercalated the account of the Institution, with the epiclesis and the anamnesis.

We pray for the Church—we name the Pope, the bishops, the priests, the deacons, and in a general way, all those who have the care of the people of God—for the dead who have preceded us in

Communion in Praise with the Saints of Heaven
Anaphora of Saint Basil

It is a commandment of your only Son, Lord, that we remember the saints. Therefore deign also to remember those who pleased you from the beginning:

—the holy fathers, patriarchs, apostles, prophets, preachers evangelists, martyrs, confessors and all the just who kept the faith of Christ until the end.

—Especially be mindful of our holy, glorious, immaculate, most blessed Lady, Mother of God and ever-Virgin Mary;

—of your holy and glorious prophet, John the Baptist, forerunner and martyr;

—of Saint Stephen, first deacon and first martyr;

—of our holy father Saint Mark, apostle and evangelist;

—of our holy father Basil, the wonder-worker;

—of Saint N. whose memory we celebrate today, and of all your choir of saints.

Through their prayers and intercession, have mercy on us and save us for the sake of your name which is invoked upon us.

according to C. Vagaggini, *Le Canon de la Messe*, p. 49.

faith and who now live next to God, for the celebrating community so that it may be gathered together with the Virgin Mary and all the saints of heaven in a single and eternal praise. The Church, communion in praise, is also communion in supplication. In this way it imitates the prayer of Jesus. Just as his praise towards his Father is also intercession for his brothers and sisters, thus our praise toward Christ opens upon an intercession for all of humanity.

Doxology:
"To the Father, through the Son, in the Holy Spirit"

Describing the Mass around the year 150, Justin relates: "When the prayer is ended, bread, wine, and water are brought up. The one who presides then prays and gives thanks accordingly to his ability, and all the people respond with the acclamation 'Amen!' "[49]

The entire Eucharistic Prayer is doxological, that is, word *(logos)* of praise *(doxa)* to God. And the *Amen* of the assembly which concludes this praise in fact ratifies the whole prayer. The doxology that terminates the Eucharistic Prayer sums up the totality of this praise.

The Roman liturgy has kept the old Trinitarian formula:

> Through him, with him, in him,
> in the unity of the Holy Spirit,
> all glory and honor is yours
> almighty Father
> for ever and ever. Amen.

Instead of simply signifying the equality of the persons in reaction against Arianism, as in the doxology "Glory to the Father, to the Son, and to the Holy Spirit," the liturgical formula underlines the relationship of the divine Persons among themselves. It responds better to the givens of the New Testament: "There is only one God and Father, from whom everything comes, and one Lord, Jesus Christ, through whom everything exists" (1 Cor 8:6). Therefore, it is right that all praise goes up to the Father through Christ.

By adding "in the unity of the Holy Spirit," the liturgy affirms the unifying power of the Spirit. Just as the Spirit is the "bond of the Trinity,"[50] as he unites the Father and the Son in Love, thus likewise, "the Spirit knits everything that is for God in the world into a doxology . . . He binds the sheaf into cosmic praise."[51]

While saying the doxology, the priest lifts up the bread and wine in a gesture of offering. In this gesture are signified the history of the world and its ultimate destiny. All of creation is born in the heart of the Father, fruit of his love. All of creation is established in existence through Christ, "the firstborn of all creation" (Col 1:15). All of creation is indwelt by the Spirit who fills it with his love. Having become the body of Christ in the bread and wine, changed into Eucharist, that is, into thanksgiving and praise, creation now

---

[49] *Apology*, 1,67, Deiss, *Springtime of the Liturgy*, p. 93.

[50] Epiphanius (†403), *Adversus Haereses Panariom*, 62,4. PG 41, 1055A.

[51] Y. Congar, *Je crois en L'Esprit Saint*, vol. II (Paris: Cerf, 1979), pp. 284, 288.

goes up to the Father. It is this movement of the universe towards the eternity of God that the gesture of the doxology signifies. It is for this history of the world, in which is found our own history, that we give glory to the Father, through the Son, in the Spirit.

3. COMMUNION RITES AND PRAYERS

"Our Father":
The Prayer of Children

The Our Father in the Tradition of the Gospels

The Our Father has come to us according to a double tradition, the one of Matt 6:9-13 and the one of Luke 11:2-4.

The liturgy has retained the Matthean version. It is divided into seven requests. The first three requests are "celestial" in the sense that they concern God: his name, his kingdom, his will.

—hallowed be thy name;
—thy kingdom come;
—thy will be done on earth as it is in heaven.

The four following requests are "terrestrial": they concern humanity.

—Give us this day our daily bread;
—forgive us our trespasses as we forgive those
—who trespass against us;
—and lead us not into temptation,
—but deliver us from evil.

The early community did not take exception to the differences that it perceived between the Matthean and the Lukan traditions, differences that had come especially from additions that Matthew had brought to the text. It thought that the Our Father is above all a spirit rather than a letter, a spiritual message rather than something to be recited word for word. The message of the Lord's Prayer is the following: According to the express will of Jesus, God wants to be called upon as Father. Jesus himself addressed God with this name of tenderness: "Abba, Father!" (Mark 14:36). The Lord's Prayer is not the request of servants to a master, but the prayer of children to their Father. "To dare to pronounce the invocation of Father is to be conscious of filiation; only children can say Abba."[52] Inversely, Jesus said, "Do not give anyone on earth the name of Father, for you have only one Father, your heavenly Father" (Matt 23:9).

This orientation towards the Father marks not only the seven requests of the Our Father, but likewise gives form to all other prayer. A prayer is Christian if it is addressed to the Father, otherwise it is not. The Eucharistic celebration itself is praise of children toward their Father in heaven.

The "Our Father" in the Eucharistic Celebration

It seems that the oldest attestation of the presence of the Our Father in the Eucharistic liturgy is read in the writings of Saint Ambrose (†397).[53] It is probable that this presence at the heart of the Eucharistic Prayer was progressively generalized.

It is clear that it is the request for daily bread that motivated this insertion. It is even possible that in its literal sense this request concerns not so much the bread of the earth—concerning which Jesus precisely asks us not to worry (Matt 6:25)—but that heavenly manna[54] which comes down from heaven and gives eternal life (John 6:32-33). Finally it is clear that the request for bread of the earth leads to the request for spiritual goods. One asks for bread; God gives his Spirit: "If you, who are evil, know how to give good gifts to your children, how much more will your Father in heaven give the Holy Spirit to those who ask him!" (Luke 11:13). And who can claim to know exactly where the request for bread ends and the request for the Holy Spirit begins?

In the Eastern Churches the Our Father was recited by the entire community as it is today. In Rome, on the contrary, in the time

---

[52] J. Jeremias, *Théologie du Nouveau Testament*, Coll. "Lectio Divina," 76 (1973), p. 247.

[53] *De Sacramentis*, V,20. SC 25 bis (1961), p. 130.

[54] See J. Carmignac, *Recherches sur le "Notre Père"* (Paris: Ed. Letouzey & Ané, 1969), pp. 118–221.

of Saint Gregory (†604) it was considered a presidential prayer. Therefore, the priest recited it alone. Undoubtedly it was Spain that had the most original custom. The priest sang the Our Father alone, and the assembly ratified each request through the acclamation of its *Amen*.

Fortunately, the Missal has restored what is the "prayer of children" par excellence to the entire Christian community.

The Embolism: "Deliver Us, Lord, from Every Evil"

A literary development from a text is called *embolism* (from the Greek *embolisma*, "piece added to a garment"). The Our Father ends with "deliver us from evil." The embolism adds: "Deliver us, Lord, from every evil . . ." This embolism seems to go back to the epoch of Saint Gregory.

Indeed, one can ask why the reform kept this piece added to the Our Father from the sixth century. Was the Lord's Prayer not enough? Was it necessary to complete the words of Jesus?

The affirmation "we wait in joyful hope for the coming of our Savior, Jesus Christ" goes back to the text of Titus 2:13: "We await the blessed hope and the coming (literally: the epiphany) of the glory of our great God and Savior, Jesus Christ." It is not a matter of a faceless goodness that we are awaiting but really the coming in glory of Jesus Christ, of the goodness that we read on the face of the risen Christ.

The Doxology of the "Our Father"

The embolism ends with the doxology:

For the kingdom, the power, and the glory are yours
now and forever.

This doxology does not belong to the text of the Lord's Prayer according to Matthew. It is found in an abridged form in the prayer of the *Didache* (pp. 63–64). It is a very old liturgical creation (first or second century). It was inserted into Matthew's text no doubt around the third century, perhaps at Antioch. It is used by the majority of the Churches of the East as well as by the Protestants and the Anglicans. By integrating it into the Roman Mass, the new Missal joins the tradition of the other Christian Churches.

According to the rubrics, the doxology that ends the Eucharistic Prayer ("Through him, with him, in him. . .") is reserved for the priest alone.[55] Here and there, a community caught up in the fervor of its participation joins in spontaneously, especially if this doxology is recited or sung by a group of concelebrating priests. Is it necessary to hold it against them for singing the glory of God? Fortunately, the doxology of the Our Father does not pose this rubrical problem, since it comes back to the entire assembly.

It is difficult to explain or to justify that, of these two doxologies recited in a moment's interval, the first is "presidential," therefore cannot be taken up by the community, while the second is not and consequently goes back to the assembly. This is a question of a rubrical curiosity. There is no good reason to be excessively troubled by it.

The true problem, in both doxologies, is to make our entire life a song of praise to the glory of the Father.

Rites Surrounding the Breaking of the Bread

The Rite of Peace

The General Instruction explains: "The faithful implore peace and unity for the Church and for the whole human family and offer some sign of their love for one another."[56]

Here one thinks quite naturally of the words of Christ: "If you present your offering at the altar and there you remember that your brother has something against you, leave your offering at the altar and go first to reconcile yourself with your brother" (Matt 5:23-24). It is in this spirit that the new Zairian rite placed the rite of peace before the bringing of the gifts for the Eucharistic liturgy.[57]

[55] Point recalled in the instruction *Inaestimabile Donum*, 4, of April 3, 1980.
[56] *General Instruction of the Roman Missal*, 56b.
[57] *Notitiae*, 264 (1988), p. 461.

The sign of peace is exchanged "pro opportunitate," according to when it is judged opportune.[58] It can be considered always opportune to signify communion in peace and mutual love. As for the sign itself, it is determined by the conference of bishops "in accord with the culture and customs of the people."[59]

The Rite of the Breaking of the Bread

The rite of the breaking of the bread renews Christ's gesture at the Last Supper. During the apostolic age, the Eucharistic celebration was called "the breaking of the bread." Paul explains: Is not the bread that we break a communion in the body of Christ? Since there is only one loaf, we all form only one body, for we all partake of one loaf (1 Cor 10:16-17).

Formerly, this rite took a long time since one had to break the consecrated bread for the entire assembly. Beginning in the thirteenth century, the rite lost some of its significance, the hosts having been prepared and cut in advance. Presently, since there is only one host to break, the one of the priest, the rite passes almost unnoticed.

The Rite of Commingling

One can say as much about the rite of commingling: the priest "drops a part of the host into the chalice."[60] The Missal does not give any explanation for this rite. We no longer see the necessity for it and we are not sure of its significance. Nevertheless it has been kept through faithfulness to tradition. Diverse explanations have been proposed.

It is supposed that originally it was a matter of *fermentum:* a piece of the Eucharistic bread from the Papal Mass was carried to the priests of the churches of Rome who, because of the service that they fulfilled for their faithful, could not attend the Papal Mass. Commingling manifested the unity of the presbyterium of Rome with the Pope.

---

[58] *General Instruction of the Roman Missal,* 112.
[59] *Ibid.,* 56b.
[60] *Ibid.,* 56d.

We can also think of the consecrated bread—called *sancta*—that was kept for the communion of the dying. When those breads became too hard, they were replaced. In order to consume them more easily, they were softened by them in consecrated wine.

A symbolic explanation was also devised. The Eucharistic bread and wine represent the body and blood of Christ. They appear separated on the altar: which represents the death of Christ. By uniting them in the cup, we signify "the resurrection that has reunited for ever, for eternal life, the soul and body of Christ."[61] Perhaps. Nevertheless, we can wonder if our good people perceive this symbolism. Upon seeing the bread and the wine on the table of the altar, we think spontaneously not of the death of Christ, but rather of a meal. It is a matter of a sign of life, not death. On the other hand, it is not our habit to dip bread in a cup of wine. In any case, the gesture is not in good taste.

During the rite, the priest used to say the following prayer: "May the commingling and consecration of the body and blood of our Lord Jesus Christ become for us who receive them eternal life." The word "consecration" created enormous problems of interpretation. Fortunately, the new Missal has omitted this prayer. The English translation reads as follows: "May this mingling of the body and blood of our Lord Jesus Christ bring eternal life to us who receive it." The French translation is very elegant: "May the body and blood of Jesus Christ, reunited in this cup, nourish eternal life in us." This prayer is said quietly[62] (*secreto*): from all evidence, one is not bound to give this rite great emphasis.

The Singing of the Agnus Dei

During the breaking of the bread, the *Agnus Dei* is sung.

The liturgical text is borrowed from the witness that John the Baptist rendered to Jesus:

> There is the Lamb of God
> who takes away the sin of the world (John 1:29).

---

[61] Le Gall, *Dictionnaire de Liturgie*, C.L.D., 1983, p. 71.
[62] *General Instruction of the Roman Missal*, 113.

The title *Lamb of God* comes no doubt from the fourth song of the Servant of Yahweh according to Deutero-Isaiah. It is said there that the Servant justifies the people by taking their sin upon himself. He is compared at the same time to a lamb that is immolated (Isa 53:6-11). The superposition of the images of the Servant and of the Lamb was easier because in Aramaic the word *talya*, "lamb," can mean at the same time "servant," "son." John the Baptist could have said: "Here is the Servant of God who takes away the sin of the world." The early community, after the resurrection, retained: "Here is the Lamb of God . . . who takes away the sin of the world." In that way it retrieved at the same time the richness of the symbolism of the paschal Lamb. This image was in great favor in the early community. The author of the First Letter of Peter affirms: "You have been redeemed . . . by the precious blood like that of a lamb without blemish or defect, Christ" (1 Pet 1:18-19). Paul can affirm, without giving other explanation: "Christ, our Passover, has been sacrificed" (1 Cor 5:7). John sees in Christ on the cross the figure of the paschal Lamb (John 19:36; Exod 12:46). Finally, the Book of Revelations speaks twenty-eight times about Christ as the paschal Lamb. This Lamb bears the stigmata of his Passion into his resurrection, but at the same time he is glorified as much as God in a doxology of seven terms:

> Worthy is the Lamb who was slain,
> to receive power, wealth, wisdom,
> strength, honor, glory and praise (Rev 5:12).

The liturgy unites the images of the Lamb-Servant and of the paschal Lamb. When presenting the Eucharistic bread to the community, the priest says:[63]

> Here is the Lamb who takes away the sin of the world.
> Happy are those who are invited
> to the wedding banquet of the Lamb! (Rev 19:9).

The beatitude: "Happy are those who are invited to the wedding banquet of the Lamb" is a literal quote of Rev 19:9. According to the Book of Revelation, the "wedding banquet of the Lamb"

---

[63] *Ordo Missae*, 133 (Latin text).

is the celebration in heaven when time will be set in eternity, of the definitive triumph of the "immense crowd" (Rev 19:1, 6) of the elect.

The English Missal did not dare to take up the image of the "wedding banquet of the Lamb" and thus adapts the biblical text: "Happy are those who are called to his supper." Therefore, it limits Revelation's invitation to the eternal celebration in God's presence to an invitation to receive Communion. Such an adaptation is regrettable. It can also be justified by thinking that, for our communities not very familiar with the vocabulary and images of Revelation, such an adaptation was no doubt useful, perhaps even necessary. Finally, we note that the readings of the Lectionary (Thursday of the Thirty-fourth Week of Ordinary Time) and those of the Divine Office (Fifth Sunday of Easter Time), respecting the text of Revelation, have kept the image of the wedding banquet of the Lamb.

In principle, the invocation *Lamb of God* is used three times, under litanic form. The General Instruction adds: "This invocation may be repeated as often as necessary to accompany the breaking of the bread."[64] This last disposition is somewhat theoretic. In practice, little hosts are generally used for the assembly and a single big host for the priest. Because of that, the rite of the breaking lasts only a moment: it is ordinarily finished before one has the time to sing the first invocation of the Lamb of God.

Therefore, we find ourselves brought back again to the very important problem concerning the symbolic domain of the truth of the signs utilized. The Missal notes very well: "The nature of the sign demands that the material for the eucharistic celebration truly have the appearance of food. Accordingly, even though unleavened and baked in the traditional shape, the eucharistic bread should be made in such a way that in a Mass with a congregation the priest is able actually to break the host into parts and distribute them to at least some of the faithful."[65]

In order to give consistency to the rite of breaking of the bread, while not prolonging it when the assembly is large, it would be desirable to have one or more loaves of bread of some importance

[64] *General Instruction of the Roman Missal*, 56e.
[65] *Ibid.*, 283.

in addition to the little hosts. The breaking would be visible by the entire assembly. Its duration would also be perceptible as a time of celebration.

Communion

"The Body of Christ! "Amen!"

In antiquity, the most usual formula for the distribution of Communion was: "The Body of Christ." The communicant responded: "Amen!" In this way he or she made a true profession of faith. Saint Augustine explains:

> If you are the body of Christ and its members, it is the sacrament of what you are which is placed on the Lord's table: it is the sacrament of what you are which you receive. It is to what you are that you respond *Amen.* This response is your signature. You hear: "Body of Christ." You respond: "Amen!" Be a member of the Body of Christ so that your Amen may be true.[66]

As it often happens, through veneration for the body of the Lord, Christian piety progressively amplified the early formula. We can cite:[67] "The holy body—the precious blood—of the Lord, our God and Savior" (Liturgy of Saint Mark). "The bread of life that comes down from heaven, the body of Christ," "The cup of life that comes down from heaven: this is the blood of Christ" (Egyptian Tradition). "This is the body of Jesus Christ. This is the blood of Jesus Christ, our Lord" (Palestinian Tradition). Around the eighth century we find the formula which, in equivalent terms, prevailed in our Roman liturgy until the reform of Vatican II: "May the body and blood of our Lord Jesus keep you for eternal life."

The multiplication of words does not multiply reverence for the Eucharist. The return to the old formula, with Communion in the hand, figures among the most successful reforms of Vatican II.

---

[66] *Sermo* 272. PL 38,1247.
[67] Brightman, *Liturgies Eastern and Western,* pp. 140, 241, 464.

Communion in the Hand

The reception of the host on the tongue was established in the ninth century.[68] Previously, the general rule was to receive the host in the hand. Cyril of Jerusalem (†387) explains to the neophytes of Jerusalem:

> When you come forward, do not draw near with your hands wide open or with your fingers spread apart; instead, with your left hand make a throne for the right hand, which will receive the King. Receive the Body of Christ in the hollow of your hand and give the response: "Amen" . . . Draw near also to the cup of his Blood. Do not stretch out your hands, but bow in adoration and respect, and say: "Amen" . . . And while your lips are still wet, touch them with your fingers and sanctify your eyes, your forehead, and your other senses. Then, while waiting for the prayer, give thanks to God who judged you worthy of such great mysteries.[69]

The custom of receiving Communion while kneeling was established progressively from the eleventh to the sixteenth centuries. The table of Communion dates from the eighteenth century.

Communion from the Chalice

Communion from the chalice was the general rule until the twelfth century. It tends today to become the universal practice each time that it is easily realizable. The Missal explains well: "Holy Communion has a more complete form as a sign when it is received under both kinds."[70]

It is possible that for diverse reasons—either hygienic or psychological—people may not want to drink directly from the cup. In that case they can use a tube to drink from the cup; this practice is attested after the eighth century. One can also receive Communion by "intinction": the consecrated bread is dipped into the

---

[68] J. A. Jungmann, *Missarum Solemnia*, vol. 3, p. 314. On pp. 306–325 you will find documentation relative to the history of communion of the faithful.

[69] *Mystagogical Catechesis*, 23, 22.—L. Deiss, *Springtime of the Liturgy*, p. 289. Concerning the authenticity of these catecheses, see pp. 270–271.

[70] *General Instruction of the Roman Missal*, 240.

chalice;[71] this custom is attested in the seventh century. All these practices are old and respectable. However, it can be noted that they lack the simplicity with which the table of the Lord should be surrounded. Jesus said: "Take this and eat it. Take this and drink it." He did not say: "Take this and dunk it."

Frequency of Communion

It has been noted that "until the fourth century, communion of the faithful was not only the rule at each Mass, but it was more frequent than the celebration of the Mass, which was limited in general to Sunday."[72] Actually, the faithful carried the Eucharist home. Hippolytus of Rome advised them to commune every day before taking any other food. The conservation of the Eucharistic bread could pose problems. Hippolytus recommended: "Let each one take care that no unbeliever, or mouse, or other animal taste the Eucharist and that no piece of the Eucharist fall on the ground or get lost. It is really the body of the Lord that the faithful eat, and it must not be scorned."[73]

From the fourth century forward, we note a rapid decline in the frequency of communion. Different factors brought about this decline. In reaction against Arianism, one underlined the redoubtable mystery, *mysterium tremendum*, of the divinity of Christ. From the tenth century forward, sacramental penitence was required before communion. Requirements of ritual purity borrowed from the Old Testament were brought forward. Saint Caesarius of Arles (†542) asked married couples who had had relations not to set foot in church for thirty days.[74] That is how the sacrament of Christ's tenderness came to be disfigured by human tradition. In the eleventh century the Church imposed communion three times a year: at Christmas, Easter, and Pentecost. At the Council of Lateran in 1215, it imposed it once a year.

[71] *Ibid.*, 243.
[72] J. A. Jungmann, *op. cit.*, vol. 3, p. 291.
[73] *Apostolic Tradition*, 36–37.
[74] *Serm.* 44 (=Pseudo-Augustin, *Serm.* 292,5).—PL 39, 2299. Cited by J. A. Jungmann, *Missarum Solemnia*, p. 295, note 23.

The Council of Trent encouraged frequent communion. Pope Pius X reestablished it effectively.

Today, due to the fact that the prayers are all in a living language, it is assumed that the faithful receive communion at each Mass.

The Communion Song

The General Instruction explains: "During the priest's and the faithful's reception of the sacrament the communion song is sung. Its function is to express outwardly the communicants' union in spirit by means of the unity of their voices, to give evidence of joy of heart, and to make the procession to receive Christ's body more fully an act of community."[75] Cyril of Jerusalem tells us that Ps 33 (34) was sung. The antiphon "Taste and see that the Lord is good" is especially suitable for expressing the Eucharistic joy of the community.

After the communal praise of the communion song, it is opportune to provide a time of silence for individual thanksgiving. This time can be concluded by "a hymn, psalm, or other song of praise."[76]

The Missal, which offers a great deal of flexibility for the organization of communion, does not specify how many songs the assembly must sing. However, a rule of common sense would say clearly: one song, either during communion or after communion, suffices in a general way to express the joy of the assembly.

It is highly desirable that the priest not pollute the time of silence after communion by "purifying" the paten and chalice at that moment. This purification has nothing to do with a celebration. No more than one would clean the kitchen or wash the dishes in front of the guests, one should not proceed with the purification while the assembly is still present. Therefore, it is with much good sense that the Missal recommends doing the purification "after the Mass when the people have left."[77]

---

[75] *General Instruction of the Roman Missal*, 56i.
[76] *Ibid.*, 56j.
[77] *Ibid.*, 120.

Prayer after Communion

In this presidential prayer God is implored to make the Eucharist that gathered us together bear fruit.

4. CONCLUDING RITES

Final Blessing

Before sending his disciples into the world to bear witness to his resurrection before all the nations, Jesus Christ, "lifting up his hands, blessed them. And while he was blessing them, he was taken up into heaven" (Luke 24:50-51). Before sending the faithful back into the world to announce the resurrection of Christ to their brothers and sisters, the priest likewise lifts up his hand over them, marks them with the sign of the cross, and invokes the blessing of

---

Prayer after the Communion of the People

We give you thanks, O Master, for having called those who were in error, for having reconciled those who had sinned. You passed over the threat that weighed upon us; through your love for humanity, you took it away; through conversion, you abandoned it; through your knowledge, you rejected it.

We give you thanks for having made us share in the body and blood (of your Son). Bless us and bless this people . . . through your only-begotten Son.

Through him glory to you and power, in the Holy Spirit, now and for ever and ever! Amen.

Anaphora of Serapion, 16 (Egypt, fourth cent.)
L. Deiss, *Springtime of the Liturgy*, p. 198.

the Father, of the Son, and of the Holy Spirit upon them.[78] The faithful had been gathered together in the church, a sanctuary of stone. Now they are going to spread out in the sanctuary which is the universe. They had been united to form a community of brothers and sisters. Now they are going to carry to their brothers and sisters in the world the cross of light with which they have been marked. They had formed a community of praise. They are going to make praise resound on the entire earth.

In her description of the liturgy in use in Jerusalem (between 381 and 384), the pilgrim Egeria reports that when the liturgical service was ended, the faithful approached the bishop and he blessed them before retiring.[79] A parallel custom existed likewise in Rome. While returning to the sacristy, the Pope blessed the faithful that he met on his passage.[80] This final blessing, at the moment when the president leaves his assembly, manifests well the bond that unites him to his community. The priest is ordained not to dominate his brothers and sisters, but to bring them the blessing on the part of God by marking them with the cross of Jesus. To tell the truth, he does not bless them himself, rather he says the prayer that asks God to bless them: "May almighty God bless you . . ." That is the humility of the priestly ministry. That is also its eminent dignity.

The Dismissal of the Assembly

In the East, the formula of dismissal is: "Go in peace" (Antioch and Egypt), or: "Let us go in peace" (Byzantium) and, a little more religiously: "Let us go in the peace of Christ" (Eastern Syria). The people respond: "In the name of the Lord."[81] That was also the formula used in the Church of Milan.

In Rome, people had a realistic and practical spirit. They used a formula of juridic character: *"Ite, missa est."* Missa (from *mittere,* to send) means dismissal (from the fourth century forward,

---

[78] In the sixth century, on the testimony of the *Ordo Antiquus Gallicanus,* 23, a final blessing was given before communion to those who were not communing and who had been invited at that time to leave the assembly.

[79] *Journal de voyage,* 24,2. SC 296 (1982), p. 236.

[80] R. Cabié, *The Eucharist,* p. 123.

[81] Brightman, *Liturgies Eastern and Western,* pp. 67, 142, 34.

missa designates the liturgical act which preceded, that is, the Mass). Therefore, *"Ite missa est"* means quite simply: "Go, this is the dismissal," as if one were saying: "Go, it is finished" or more seriously: "Go, the meeting is concluded."[82]

Fortunately, the French Missal was inspired by the formula of Eastern Syria: "Go in the peace of Christ." The English Missal does the same. It unites the East with Rome by proposing further: "The Mass is ended, go in peace!" Finally, it adds a third, very beautiful formula: "Go in peace to love and serve the Lord!"

The priest venerates the altar one last time by kissing it. The liturgy of Antioch proposes a very moving formula of farewell:

> Rest in peace, holy altar of the Lord. I do not know if I will ever come back to you or not. May the Lord grant me to see you in the assembly of the firstborn which is in heaven; in this covenant, I place my trust. Rest in peace, holy and propitiatory altar. May the holy body and propitiatory blood that I received from you be for the forgiveness of my transgressions, the remission of my sins, and my assurance before the redoubtable tribunal of our Lord and God for ever. Rest in peace, holy altar, table of life, and beseech our Lord Jesus Christ for me so that I may not cease to think of you henceforth and for ever and ever. Amen.[83]

---

[82] R. Cabié, *The Eucharist*, p. 123.
[83] Archdale A. King, *Liturgie d'Antioche*, Mame, 1967, p. 138. Cf. Brightman, *Liturgies Eastern and Western*, p. 109.

Conclusion

While going through the Mass, we have kept an open eye on the biblical and patristic tradition as well as on the reforms that the Missal proposes to us today.

Some think that these reforms were too timid, that they devoted excessive veneration to the past, that they lacked courage in the face of the future. Others think that these reforms were too audacious, that they threw everything into disorder without retaining the venerable traditions of the old prayers. Others think wisely that these reforms were placed in a right milieu between what was ideally desirable and, at that time, peacefully realizable.

It remains that no reform is eternal. The *perennis reformatio*, the permanent reform that Vatican II speaks about,[44] is the constant duty of the Church. Among the domains in which this constant renovation must be exercised, the Council explicitly mentions the liturgy. Vatican II gave new and pertinent answers to the problems that were posed around the years 1963–1965. Since that time, especially since 1968, which is a key date which marks an acceleration in the evolution of society, the cultural environment in which Christians live has evolved with dizzying speed. The frequentation of Sunday Masses likewise evolved, but diminishing, at the same speed. That the number of Christians in certain countries like the United States does not cease to increase and the Sunday practice

---

[44] *Decree on Ecumenism,* 6.

in these same countries does not cease to diminish poses some questions. Half the Christians at the present time, more precisely those who were born ten years before the Council, do not know the Latin liturgy that existed before the Council, and therefore are familiar only with the "new" liturgy. It is less the reform of the liturgy that interests them than its present form. In the midst of old problems that have not yet received a satisfying solution, new problems have arisen. We think principally of the problems of inculturation and of acculturation of the message of Christ and of its celebration. "The dialogue of the Church and cultures assumes a vital importance for the future of the Church and of the world."[85] Do we know how to show our brothers and sisters that Christ loves them just as they are? Do we know how to draw them into celebrating this love with us?

The old prophecy from the Book of Isaiah: "I am going to create Jerusalem 'Joy' and its people 'Gladness' " (Isa 65:18) is the light that guides the Church in this permanent reform. The measure of joy and peace that each celebration brings to us is the criterion of its success.

Blessed the community which has joy as the principle rubric of its liturgy! Which, when it celebrates the Word, encounters the face of the risen Christ on each page of the Bible! Which, when it shares the bread and wine of the Eucharist, shares at the same time the love between brothers and sisters! Which, to preside over its celebration, has a priest not to dominate, but to serve!

The Mass is the heart of the Christian community. The beauty of each Mass is the beauty of Christ in our life.

[85] *La foi et l'inculturation*, 4. Document of the International Theological Commission, DC 86 (1989), p. 281.

Glossary

AGAPE—Greek, *love*. Signifies the meal of the first Christians, meant to symbolize charity and Christian unity. This meal usually preceded the Eucharistic celebration.

AGNUS DEI—Latin which means *Lamb of God*. Title given to Christ by the early community. A song which accompanies the rite of the breaking of the bread.

ALLELUIA—From the Hebrew, *Halelû-Yah*, which means "Praise the Lord" (Yahweh).

AMBO—From Greek *anabainein*, "to go up." The place, usually elevated, from where the Word of God is proclaimed.

AMEN—Hebrew which means "So be it" or "Thus may it be so."

ANAMNESIS—From Greek meaning "to remember." Prayer after the consecration where we remember the death and the Resurrection of Jesus. See p. 84.

ANAPHORA—From Greek meaning an *offering* (literally: elevation, referring to the sacrifice offered or lifted up to God). In Eastern Liturgies, this word indicates the Eucharistic Prayer. See p. 61.

CANON—Latin meaning a *ruler*. In the ancient Roman liturgy, refers to the Eucharistic Prayer. See p. 61.

COLLECT—Prayer of the presider of the assembly which "collects" the prayer of all gathered into one prayer. See pp. 28–30.

CREDO—Latin meaning "I believe." Profession of faith which is said immediately after the Gospel and homily.

DEUTERO-ISAIAH—Second part of the book of the prophet Isaiah (chapters 40–55), attributed to a disciple of the tradition of Isaiah, dating to the years 550 B.C.

DIDACHE—Greek meaning *teaching*. Refers to the oldest Christian "manual." It possibly dates back to the Apostolic Period (during the years 60's A.D., according to J.-P. Audet) or in its totality to the first century of the Common Era (see *Sources Chretiennes*, 248, p. 96). The complete title reads *The Didache (the Teaching) of the Twelve Apostles.*

DOXOLOGY—From Greek *doxa*, "praise" and *logos*, "word." Prayer where one proclaims the glory of God. See pp. 87–88.

EGERIA (sometimes Etheria)—A Christian woman who made a pilgrimage to the Holy Land around 381–384, whose travel journal we possess. This journal supplies us with a large number of details about the Christian liturgy as it was celebrated in the churches of Palestine.

EPICLESIS—From Greek *klēsis*, "invocation" and *epi*, "over." Prayer which invokes the sending of the Holy Spirit on the bread and the wine. See pp. 73–74.

ESCHATOLOGY—Discourse *(logos)* on the end times *(eschaton)*.

EUCHARIST—From Greek *eucharistia*, meaning a "thanksgiving." Refers first to the prayer of thanksgiving which is said over the bread and the wine, then in the middle of the second century, it came to mean the bread and the wine themselves over which the prayer was said. See p. 62.

EVANGELIARY—Liturgical book containing only the Gospels. See pp. 36–37.

GLORIA—Latin indicating a hymn of "Glory to God," sung at the beginning of Mass. See pp. 23–25.

HIPPOLYTUS OF ROME—(circa 170-236), priest of the Church of Rome. Among his numerous theological works, his *Apostolic Tradition* (circa 215) presents the most ancient Eucharistic Prayer. See pp. 41–43.

HOMILY—From Greek *homilia*, "reunion," or a family meeting. The homily is the discourse which translates and actualizes the Word of God.

INSTITUTION—The Institutional Narratives are the biblical texts which recount the action of Jesus at the Last Supper, when he instituted the Eucharist saying, "Do this in memory of me." See pp. 78–80.

KYRIE ELEISON—Greek text from the Gospel which means "Lord, have mercy." See pp. 19–23.

LECTIONARY—Book which contains the readings of the Word of God for liturgical use.

MASS—From Latin *missa*, "emissary," from the verb *mittere*, "to send." *Missa est* literally means "It is the sending forth." *Missa* later came to mean the totality of the liturgical celebration preceding the sending forth. See pp. 102–103.

OBLATION—From Latin *oblatus*, meaning an offering for the celebration of the Mass, that is the bread and the wine for the Eucharist. See pp. 49–55, 59–61.

OFFERTORY—Prayers and rites which in the ancient Mass accompanied the offering of the unconsecrated bread and the wine. The liturgical reform of Vatican II has changed the ancient offering into the "Preparation of the Gifts." See pp. 49–51.

ORDO—(Understand *ordo missae*, "the order of the Mass") The book which specifies the order for the celebration of the Mass. See pp. 14–15.

PAROUSIA—Greek word meaning "presence." Indicates the coming of Christ at the end of time.

POST-SANCTUS—Prayer which follows the Sanctus, beginning with the words "You are truly holy." See p. 75.

PREFACE—First prayer of the Eucharistic liturgy strictly speaking. It is said *(fateri)* by the priest before *(prae)* the community, as a solemn prologue to the Eucharist. See pp. 70–71.

SANCTUS—The "Holy, Holy, Holy" sung after the Preface.

SHEMA ISRAEL—Prayer in the Jewish tradition which starts with the words, "Hear, O Israel," according to the text of Deuteronomy 6:4.

TRISAGION—Song which repeats three times *(tris)* the acclamation Holy *(hagios)*.

YAHWEH—Name of God which appears in the biblical translations. The original text has only the consonants YHWH with no vowels, making the pronunciation very uncertain.

Bibliography

F. E. Brightman. *Liturgies Eastern and Western* I. *Eastern Liturgies*. Oxford: Clarendon Press, 1896.

R. Cabie. *The Eucharist.* The Church at Prayer 2. Edited by A. G. Martimort and translated by M. J. O'Connell. Collegeville, Minn.: The Liturgical Press, 1986.

L. Deiss. *Springtime of the Liturgy.* Translated by M. J. O'Connell. Collegeville, Minn.: The Liturgical Press, 1967.

A. Hänggi and I. Pahl. *Prex Eucharistica.* Fribourg: Editions Universitaires, 1968).

International Commission on English in the Liturgy (ICEL). *Documents on the Liturgy, 1963–1979: Conciliar, Papal, and Curial Texts.* Collegeville, Minn.: The Liturgical Press, 1982.

J. A. Jungmann. *Missarum Sollemnia.* 3 vols. Vienna: Herder Verlag, 1949. English text: *The Mass of the Roman Rite.* 2 vols. Translated by F. A. Brunner. Westminster, Md.: Christian Classics, 1986.

R. Kaczynski. *Enchiridion Documentorum Instaurationis Liturgicae* I (1963–1973). Turin: Marietti, 1976.

CPSIA information can be obtained
at www.ICGtesting.com
Printed in the USA
FFOW02n0655280115
10658FF